How to Hide Your Cat From the Landlord

A practical and spiritual guide to living in harmony with a compatible feline in smaller spaces

by Jasmine Kinnear
**Successful Cat Breeder,
Feline Behavior Consultant and
Cattery Management & Marketing Mentor**

CCB Publishing
British Columbia, Canada

How to Hide Your Cat From the Landlord: A practical and spiritual guide to living in harmony with a compatible feline in smaller spaces

Copyright ©2006 by Jasmine Kinnear
ISBN-10   0-9739050-7-7
ISBN-13   978-0-9739050-7-6
Second Edition

Library and Archives Canada Cataloguing in Publication

Kinnear, Jasmine, 1953-
How to hide your cat from the landlord : a practical and spiritual guide
to living in harmony with a compatible feline in smaller spaces / written
by Jasmine Kinnear. -- 2nd ed.
Also available in electronic format.
ISBN 0-9739050-7-7
1. Cats. 2. Cats--Behavior. 3. Cats--Psychology. I. Title.
SF442.K55 2006   636.8   C2006-901438-8

Publisher: CCB Publishing
                British Columbia, Canada
                e-mail: info@confessionsofacatbreeder.com

Web site

www.confessionsofacatbreeder.com

Dedication

This book is dedicated with great love and affection
to my sister Pat in Corby, North Hamptonshire, England.

A lifetime separated by miles
but forever joined in matters of the heart.

With all my love,

Jasmine

~~To some blind souls all cats are much alike. To a cat lover every cat from the beginning of time has been utterly and amazingly unique~~ Jenny De Vries

Table of Contents

Introduction

This book provides a practical approach to assist everyone in the pursuit of owning a feline. Some readers will be seeking advice to keep a kitten content in their smaller homes. Others may be coping with the stress of concealing their feline's presence within their condos or apartments. It is my desire to provide answers and solutions to satisfy readers in these and other closely related situations. You will be exposed to detailed information regarding rental properties and will discover how to recognize those unique felines with personalities that are best suited to apartment life. **How to Hide Your Cat From The Landlord** is a practical and spiritual guide to living in harmony with a compatible feline in smaller spaces.

The first edition of this publication was written and published several years ago with the assistance of my former webmaster. Following numerous requests on our Confessions of a Cat Breeder web site we realized there was little information available on this important cat related subject. My notes were drafted into the original document appropriately entitled "How to Hide Your Cat From the Landlord." Now given the opportunity to fully address and expand on the material our second edition will be more complete and written in greater detail. Following requests from our valued readers I wish to enhance on this popular area of interest and further elaborate on additional issues that surface within the feline/renting scenario.

Having concealed my feline family for over 30 years I have acquired an expertise with this subject matter. While reading this publication you will discover that my approach differs from those found in other cat related books. As a Feline Behavior Consultant, I have assembled a combination of intriguing and useful facts relating to those renting and unable to part with a beloved cat. For others wishing to welcome a kitten or an adult feline into their home I also address these areas with insights gained from my years as a Registered Cat Breeder. Additionally, with this information you will have the necessary confidence to remain content while residing with your feline in a rental property.

There are two likely scenarios involved when hiding your cat from the Landlord:

1) Presently you own a cat and wish to move into a pet restricted residence.
2) Your current home has a 'pet restriction' clause but it is your desire to welcome a feline into your life.

Cat lovers in a long-term relationship with their pet will encounter unknown issues when first concealing their feline in a rental property. If you have been renting your home for an extended period and are now seeking feline companionship we advise of many details that should be addressed prior to your kitten's homecoming. Providing daily care for your kitten will simply become an addition to your present routine. Should you wish to welcome a kitten into your life and presently reside in a pet restricted residence then consider your journey started by reading this publication. Every cat has a story with each owner encountering a unique experience.

Having lived with both adult felines and new kittens in various rental properties I have acquired personal knowledge of many situations confronting tenants. You will discover how to cope with the daily stresses involved when hiding your cat and how to minimize them. With a new kitten you can expect various changes to occur within your household. We suggest how you may adjust your current lifestyle to benefit your personal well-being and that of your treasured cat. The adoption of a grieving feline following the loss of their owner will also be examined. If you are residing in a rental home with pet restrictions you may have conflicting emotions regarding such a commitment.

I unexpectantly inherited two domestic felines from a dear friend following her death. With time I came to appreciate how deeply cats remain committed to their original owner when such a loss occurs. Everyone processes grief in an unique manner and the same time sensitivity should be respected while coping with a grieving feline. When establishing your own relationship with a feline experiencing loss there remains a delicate emotional balance that must be respected before any bonding may occur. Whether or not you have the advantage of an established relationship with an inherited cat this publication will provide assistance to encourage a successful bonding. Felines do grieve and will react when a beloved owner appears to have abandoned them. This information will assist you in understanding cats during such a transitional time and explain how to establish your own intimate bond with them.

We will be presenting selected information from our Felines by Design series of publications. This will further assist to ease your transition when residing with a feline in a rental property. The concept of a compatible kitten for each buyer became the foundation of how kittens were sold in my cattery. It's imperative to learn the right method to locate a healthy and compatible kitten or adult domestic or purebred feline. By incorporating our Felines by Design principles you will have the knowledge to select the perfect feline personality for your situation. Some cats are specifically suited for residing in smaller spaces such as apartments, townhouses and condominiums. We affectionately refer to these felines as being the Perfect Condo Kitty. Finally, we also advise which designer personalities are best suited for quiet feline companionship.

~~One small cat changes coming home to an empty house to coming home~~ Pam Brown

Jasmine's Story of Feline Concealment

My experience with feline concealment began when I rented a small house from my friend's parents who lived several miles away. Fortunately the subject of pets was never discussed when the house was first viewed. I thought the less said the better and with no contract signed I was accepted as the new tenant. I introduced my three pet cats and was finally able to provide my hidden treasures with additional freedom of movement in a larger space.

As a writer of artistic temperament I confess to periods of time when I am overly sensitive. Therefore never knowing when the Landlord would intrude upon our privacy I was always prepared. As the years passed I knew chances were the presence of my cats would eventually be realized. However due to continued diligence and careful precautions over a 30-year span of residing in apartments, condos and duplexes this fear never materialized. Even during the transfer of ownership of our home and the additional stress of new Landlords we were never discovered.

Although some may view this presentation as deceitful this isn't how I have chosen to live my life. I was faced with a set of circumstances and simply could not bear losing my cats. Therefore I considered myself blessed and was prepared to live within my limited boundaries. While the Landlord was never aware of my cats I spent a great deal of time enduring additional costs in caring for the house. The previous tenants had been evicted because they were selling drugs from the premises. As a result even though the Landlord had known me for many years I was aware that the neighbors were watching my home carefully. I kept the outside grounds well maintained and the property clean never providing my neighbors with any cause to complain.

Inside, my house was immaculately clean and the carpets remained sanitary. Guests to our home were questioned if they were able to detect the presence of my cats. I was usually informed that there was no visible evidence typical of felines residing in a house. My cats provided such wealth to my life that although there was additional work I have never regretted my decision. Despite the stress I believe residing with my beloved cats gave my life greater purpose and they were well worth any additional expense. I was a single mother with very little money. However my rent was always paid on time and I never complained about anything that needed to be addressed on the property. If I wasn't able to make a repair myself then I paid for a professional and never troubled my Landlord.

Yes, I hid my cats. Despite how challenging the life of a single mother may become my cats were my salvation and my life would have been empty without them. In appreciation for my Landlord's trust I was the model tenant. Over time as that trust became established my Landlord remained comfortable with our rental agreement and I was seldom contacted. Considering I was not following all the rules I always made sure they were pleased with every aspect of my tenancy.

After five years I was comfortable within my rental surroundings to begin my life's purpose of breeding purebred felines. Over many years my cattery produced countless litters of kittens with several stud males and many breeding queens. I encountered few problems despite the number of felines living within our premises. My good fortune is credited to always being prepared, organized and never providing my Landlord with any reason to complain. Therefore I am addressing this subject as both a Feline Behavior Consultant and Registered Cat Breeder having acquired years of experience by living with felines in seclusion.

~~With the qualities of cleanliness, affection, patience, dignity and courage that cats have, how many of us, I ask you, would be capable of becoming cats?~~ Fernand Mery

Examining Various
Living Accommodations

Some tenants are required to hide a feline with whom they have established a long and intimate relationship. In such a situation your greatest advantage is the knowledge of your cat's personal idiosyncrasies. By sharing a loving relationship you are well aware of their noise and current activity levels. Therefore you may be reasonably certain if they will comfortably adapt to living in relative seclusion.

There are times in life when circumstances dictate a move. The loss of a spouse or of a significant relationship through death or divorce may determine a change in finances. As a result, often during an emotional crisis a change of residence will become a necessity. Confronting such a difficult situation should not have to include losing a beloved cat. Hence many people may be faced with renting for the first time and also being placed in a situation where hiding their cat is a necessity for their emotional health.

Consider your finances. Are you restricted to apartment life? Are you able to purchase a condo or is the rental of a townhouse within your financial budget? We will fully examine both the advantages and disadvantages when residing within these and other types of living accommodations.

Apartments

Apartment living may be a satisfying experience for both feline and owner. Depending on the availability of rental accommodations it need not prove impossible to locate a reasonably priced apartment. Although every city will fluctuate in cost there are solutions for every tenant's situation.

It may require additional effort to locate the appropriate apartment for residing comfortably with your feline. Over the years it has remained my personal belief that in life "you only keep what you give away." To keep your precious cat any work and expense required will be well worth your time and effort. When you have been blessed with a loving feline her comforting presence will only continue to enrich your life.

My mother has never quite understood my passion or the great comfort I have realized by living with my cats. Even though she has confided her desire to eventually own a cat she complains she can't abide the loss of their fur. However, true cat lovers consider a feline's shedding coat as simply a part of life when residing with cats. I would patiently remind my mother that despite a little more work, grooming my cats was another treasured moment in our daily relationship. It was well worth the time and effort because my attention was returned with their love and affection. Therefore when incurring additional costs to include a beloved cat while renting, consider how much comfort she offers to your life. With everything considered you would still be obligated to manage the cost of renting an apartment had you decided to live without her.

~~How you behave toward cats here below determines your status in Heaven~~ Richard A. Heinlein

Selecting an Apartment

The size of your building may actually provide additional privacy. In a high rise residence with a greater number of tenants you become one of many and your presence is not as noticeable. The placement of your apartment within the building is of the utmost importance as it may have a direct effect on your personal stress level and hence the behavior of your cat.

If you are moving to a new apartment it simply makes sense to rent as far away from the Manager as possible. Do not accept an apartment on the lower floors or at the front of the building. Some larger high rise buildings contain apartments not only on the front and back but more preferably along both sides of the building. If there are no streets on one side of the building those apartments will be rewarded with greater privacy. If such a location is unavailable another preferable location would be facing a parking lot. People returning home from work are seldom looking up into windows. If you are located a good distance from the elevator and situated at the far end of a hall, fewer people will be passing your door. It is also mandatory that you only accept an apartment where the building provides a controlled entrance. Many larger high rise apartments are also equipped with video surveillance for additional security. Tenants are able to view all visitors on their cable television prior to permitting entry into the building.

Choosing to reside at higher levels may allow you to provide your feline with indoor window ledge access. It is best to be aware of street visibility from every window ledge within your suite. It is also mandatory to screen all windows within your apartment to protect your cat. There are many choices of screens available that will not be visible from the street below. A lighter colored cat may be difficult to identify against a lightly colored drape lining. Conversely, a darker colored cat may be more difficult to detect against the darkness of a drapeless window in the evening. Should you be concerned regarding your feline's visibility from any of your windows place an object approximately the same size and color as your cat on the ledges. Having observed from various positions on the street below you'll know if other tenants in the building may detect your feline.

When provided with an opportunity, have a friend remain in your suite to place your cat on each of the ledges while you watch from the street below. Remain in contact with your friend by cell phone and provide instructions as to the placement of your feline within each window. This exercise should be repeated in daylight and during the dark of night viewing the drapes in both an open and drawn position. If you were in doubt this exercise will prove the deciding factor if your feline may be permitted the luxury of sun bathing on your window ledges. Should you be required to prevent your cat from accessing window ledges consider purchasing a tall scratching pole with sleeping ledges. Place the pole near a window and your cat will have the opportunity to exercise with a safe and private view. Indoor non-toxic potted plants or assorted knick-knacks should occupy your window ledges to both prevent and discourage your feline from gaining access to an off limits area.

The Manager

Apartments may be listed through the internet, in your local newspaper or through rental agencies in your community. It appears professional and less intrusive to make your initial contact with the Manager by telephone. Only arrange for an appointment should there be suites available that appear suitable for your lifestyle and the comfort of your feline.

In selecting your apartment building it is best to be warm and friendly but professional in your initial presentation. When dealing with Managers use your listening skills as their character will become evident if you permit them to speak. Managers or Superintendants have routinely shown apartments and therefore have a tendency to make their initial evaluation within the first ten minutes of your meeting. If you are well spoken and well dressed your character will be assessed as acceptable. Their concern will then center on providing details regarding the various attributes of the building including management's rules and regulations.

Should you be comfortable with the Manager's character your concern should then focus on viewing as many suites as are available within the building. If you indicate a preference for apartments on the side or back and on the higher floors they will have an idea of which apartments may interest you. The time of year will usually determine the number of vacancies a building may be trying to fill. Some rentals only provide a month to month tenancy while others may offer a yearly lease agreement. However should you find the perfect building without a suitable apartment inquire of any possible vacancies in the near future and request to be included on their waiting list. When you appear to be a pleasant person whom the Manager believes will create few problems more doors will be opened to you.

Keep a journal in your vehicle to make immediate note of every apartment viewed. Record where you would be most comfortable renting and include your initial impression of the Manager. Your primary concern should be the placement of your apartment and the Manager's personality. Some of them are difficult while others are simply performing their job with little interest in those tenants who are quiet. It is best to rely on your instincts as a guide regarding the Manager and your final decision whether or not to rent within that building.

If management changes while you are in residence your name should not be mentioned when you have been a pleasant tenant. The atmosphere of a building may fluctuate with much depending on the personality of the new Manager. However as a quiet, respectful tenant that seldom makes demands you will be rewarded with privacy. When providing postdated checks you eliminate any worry of neglecting to pay your rent on time or troubling your Manager with a need to knock on your door.

When attempting to hide your cat's presence in your apartment you never want to be identified as a cat lover. Therefore even if you have a large collection of cat t-shirts and jewellery it's best they not be worn in the common areas of your apartment building. It remains mandatory that management never connects you with felines. Do not display your love for cats by wearing a cat lover's ensemble of various items. I personally own countless pieces of cat jewellery, sweaters and t-shirts which I always covered with my seasonal coats and hats. It's simply better to never have your passion for cats be recognized. The less the Manager knows about you the better.

When researching this publication several cat loving Managers were also interviewed. One memorable contact was a married couple providing professional management for an exclusive 30 floor high rise apartment building. For many years they had successfully hidden their two cats from almost nine hundred tenants. Despite the constant interruptions at their front door they were extremely successful and never encountered any problems.

My initial contact was as a consultant to assist the couple in acquiring a purebred registered Sphynx kitten. I seized the opportunity to conduct an interview to fully comprehend the Landlords' perspective on this sensitive issue. Landlords seldom provide their true feelings regarding responsible tenants hiding cats in their apartments. As the building's management they were willing to share their experiences and confided their suspicions of several tenants currently hiding their felines. Bob appeared to be more troubled by disruptive and demanding tenants than those quietly living with their cats. In the position of Manager it was his responsibility to uphold the established building policy of "No Pets." However once he became aware of a good tenant hiding a feline the confidential information remained with him and was never reported. Bob further confirmed that those tenants owning cats provided the least amount of grief to his working day. Although obligated by the Building Corporation to report those not abiding by such regulations, when it came to his good tenants he would remain silent. His wife Joanne also preferred cat owners as their tenancy was usually long-term. It became her experience that tenants residing with cats left their suites in immaculate condition once they vacated the building. She believed it was in unspoken gratitude to the Managers for permitting a beloved feline the privilege of living in a "No Pets" apartment.

I have met several Managers also residing in pet restricted buildings who have further supported this sentiment. Not every Manager will claim to love cats however without exception they all prefer quiet non-demanding tenants who always pay their rent on time.

~~The cat has complete emotional honesty, human beings, for one reason or another, may hide their feelings, but a cat does not.~~ Ernest Hemingway

Maintaining Privacy & Security

There are a few simple things everyone should do to ensure their personal security. If a peep hole is not installed in your front door before taking occupancy inquire if the Manager will install one as a security precaution. Once provided with a method to view a visitor it then becomes your prerogative whether or not to permit entry. This will also provide adequate time to remove your cat, all cat toys and any other signs of a feline in residence that may be visible prior to allowing entry into your home.

It also remains a sound security practice to always shred any correspondence displaying your name, address or other pertinent information. Never provide a link to your apartment by placing bank statements, credit card bills or other confidential printed material in your building's trash or recycling facilities.

The Key to Your Personal Security

Following life in my condominium I eventually moved across town to the top floor of a high rise apartment building. Over a period of five years I rented my one bedroom suite and finally realized a life of total bliss and contentment with my cat

Dustin. Although not located in the best area of town the building provided a warm environment in which I felt totally safe and protected. In retrospect, considering my age at the time, I wasn't overly concerned with safety issues. I loved my home and felt secure by simply practicing the accepted safety precautions of many single young women.

On Friday evenings I would follow a weekly routine of transporting all my laundry downstairs to the basement during the dinner hour. One great advantage of apartment life is living in a large building where you have the use of multiple machines. I timed my laundry duties to coincide with the dinner hour to avoid encountering a busy laundry room.

The only time I left my apartment door unlocked was for the twenty minutes or so it took to transport my clean laundry back upstairs to my suite. With my apartment door locked it was difficult to balance my laundry basket and assorted items on hangers when opening the door. This system had worked for several years and remained the only time my home was left vulnerable with Dustin alone in residence.

On one particular Friday evening I was totally unprepared for a memorable encounter which was to occur behind my unlocked door. I took the elevator to the top floor while balancing a large basket of clean laundry. However, a surprise was waiting for me in my apartment. As the door swung open, I discovered a naked man lying on the floor stretched out in total comfort watching television. We stared at each other speechless in complete shock. I glanced back at the suite number displayed on the door which confirmed this was not my apartment. I quickly realized my error as I had obviously caught the elevator to the wrong floor. Thoughtlessly I intruded on a new neighbor on the floor directly beneath my own apartment who had also left his door unlocked. I stammered an apology and red faced with embarrassment shut the naked man's door retreating to the safety of my own suite directly above.

That was the last time I ever left my door unlocked for any reason. I'm sure my male neighbor residing in his suite below also learned the same valuable lesson. The moral of this story is to always keep your door locked no matter how short the duration you plan to remain outside your home. Whether getting your mail, doing your laundry or disposing of trash this essential practice should be followed at all times. In addition it is equally important to keep your door locked at all times when you are inside your apartment. This was a lesson well learned and an error in judgement I never repeated.

Years later I was informed by a client who had purchased two kittens from my cattery that she had also made this classic error. After leaving her apartment door unlocked for several minutes her two beloved six-month-old kittens were stolen from her suite. The whereabouts of the Persians were never discovered and the theft became an inconsolable and devastating loss to their owner. The story of these dear kittens was passed on whenever I sold to anyone living in an apartment or condominium. I would warn those buyers how quickly kittens or adult cats can be taken from a suite when the door has been left unlocked. Therefore for your own safety and the safety of your feline, the most valuable *key to your personal security* is to always use your key.

Purchasing & Transporting Feline Supplies

In order to maintain your privacy consistent care is also necessary when transporting feline supplies into your suite. Should your apartment provide adequate storage space, litter need not prove too difficult a challenge. Once purchased but prior to transporting home, place the cat litter bag within a non-transparent larger bag to be transferred privately to your suite. Although larger quantities of cat litter are economical they are also heavy and more difficult to handle. It should prove easier to manage the weight of litter with the use of a collapsible shopping cart. By using a shopping cart with wheels litter may then be safely transported from the car to your apartment. With the convenience of maintaining a larger supply of cat litter at home there would be fewer trips transporting it through the common areas of your building. The same cart may then serve a dual purpose as the ideal storage space for holding cat litter in your suite when kept within a closet. In place of a shopping cart I have also used a large suitcase as it could easily hold a large bag of cat litter. As the suitcase was equipped with wheels and a strong pull strap there was little difficulty transporting the contents privately to my apartment.

Although more costly you may prefer to purchase litter in more convenient smaller sizes. You will then be able to transport your cat's litter supplies through the common areas of the building with discretion. To avoid frequent trips to your pet store purchase several smaller bags of litter each time you require supplies. By enclosing these smaller bags within durable cloth shopping bags all contents will remain hidden. Ensure the contents are not visible and completely disguised while you are transporting the enclosed bags into your apartment. The same precautions should be employed when transporting cat food into your suite.

Disposal Methods

Care should also be employed when disposing of all soiled cat litter and cat food containers including bags, pails, tins, etc. The correct method used will depend on your building's refuse facilities. If you have purchased cat food and litter in paper bags or cardboard boxes then these should be shredded. Should you be unable to shred these bags or boxes then they could be reversed and used as trash bags or placed in recycling bins where facilities exist. Likewise, if you purchase litter in heavy duty plastic bags these too should be reversed and may be used as trash bags. Some companies use plastic containers for litter or dried cat food. Labels should be removed and shredded. Then place the plastic containers with your regular household waste or recycling for disposal. Similarly, when disposing of rinsed cat food tins simply remove and shred the cat identifying label then place the tins with your regular household waste or in the recycling bin.

Dispose of soiled litter frequently to prevent the bag from breaking due to the concentrated weight. Maintain a supply of standard paper bags which can be reinforced by placing them within plastic grocery bags. Both are provided when purchasing groceries and offer additional protection for litter disposal. However should your pet store supply a brand name cat litter that is flushable you may be spared additional work and not require your building's refuse facilities. Please note that it is **essential** to request at time of purchase if the store will **guarantee** that their disposible litter will **not** create plumbing hazards in your apartment suite.

Catnip Corner

Take time to prepare a special area of isolation for your cat that may be used should the Manager unexpectantly arrive at your door. It is best to own two cat carriers. One should be stored in the trunk of your car and a second that never leaves your bedroom closet. As the cat carrier in your closet is never used for transportation to the vet, you will not be stressing your feline with an environment that is associated with change and fear. The carrier in your bedroom closet should be a place of comfort associated with pleasant memories. Catnip should be placed in the carrier infrequently to encourage your cat to associate that area as part of their personal territory. Some felines are attracted to a quiet dark area where they are able to rest and will frequently retreat to the peace and quiet of their carriers.

Should you have a visitor at your door never attempt to keep your cat occupied by using catnip. This product should be used infrequently and only to associate the carrier as a feline friendly environment. Cats often become more aggressive when they are provided with catnip. With time and as your feline ages you will be better able to interpret your cat's expected behavior while he is under the influence. It should also be noted that kittens may not show any interest in catnip and some adult cats are only mildly stimulated by it's effects.

Many felines become lethargic and will sleep when they have been fed <u>pure</u> chicken or beef baby food in their secluded carriers. Make the carrier as comfortable as possible with a pillow and an article of your own clothing. **<u>Due to heat during certain times of the year</u>**, the placement of the carrier may need to be changed if the bedroom closet is deemed inappropriate. If you utilize a fan and quietly play music behind the closed bedroom door it will provide additional background noise. In fact your visitor may quickly leave as it might be assumed you are entertaining a guest in the room.

There may be circumstances when your feline must remain quietly entertained in their carrier for a short period of time. I have found it most effective to keep a sealed jar of <u>pure meat</u> baby food with a spoon and plate right in the bedroom where the carrier is kept. If the baby food is sealed and has never been opened, it can be safely stored in your bedroom for the appropriate time when it will be needed. Once opened should your cat not finish the food it must be refrigerated or safely discarded. There are assorted flavors of baby food with many including vegetables and meat. It is important to **<u>only</u>** purchase the <u>pure meat</u> variety of baby food selecting either chicken or beef according to your cat's personal preference. This food should be considered as a special treat and only opened to keep the cat occupied in his carrier while you are dealing with any unexpected company. Empty the entire jar of baby food on a plate and place it in the carrier with your cat. Keep the carrier door closed, leave the closet door ajar and close the door to your bedroom. Providing comforting music in the room will soothe the feline and also provide a background distraction to hide any sounds the cat may make in their enclosed carrier.

Chicken or beef baby food is such a pure source of meat it truly is a seductive food for cats. If only provided when you require them to be quiet they usually remain preoccupied while consuming their treat. It may be wise to practice several times to ascertain exactly how long your cat will remain quiet and if the baby food is an appropriate distraction to amuse your cat.

You may discover that the catnip corner is not an appropriate distraction for your cat. There are some felines that remain more content when they are placed and carried within their owner's favorite handbag. Even with an unexpected visitor's presence some felines are perfectly content and will stay quiet in an oversized handbag while their owner carries the bag over one shoulder. By leaving the top of the bag open and stroking their cat's fur through the unzipped opening many felines remain content with a minimal amount of contact. Caterina, my Seal Point Himalayan was always quiet as long as I had my hand inside the bag and was stroking her. Such a large handbag can also be used to quietly transport your feline through the common areas of your building to a vehicle when you both must leave the apartment. The best method employed will depend entirely on the personality and age of your feline.

Moving in with a Roommate

If you are able to move next door to a trustworthy friend there will be a safe haven for your cat should your apartment need repairs beyond your own capabilities. It can be a mutually advantageous relationship when you both have cats and are able to emotionally support one another. Should you both be seeking kittens and live side by side in the same building it is best to select litter mates who will grow and play together on a regular basis.

Try keeping the kittens in the same apartment for company during the day while you are both working. This eliminates boredom as they will adapt to each home when you rotate between the two apartments on a regular basis. By adopting this practice neither cat will become territorial and will be company for each other as they accept the other's scent and presence. Although trust is a necessity for this arrangement to succeed good friends are able to enjoy the best of both worlds. The cats will provide company for each other and not be lonely during the day. In the evenings each cat will desire their owner's presence in their own apartment. When you have a feline friendly second apartment you can share the responsibility of hiding your cat in a moment's notice.

If you are involved in a relationship or residing with a roommate then hiding your cat may prove to be less stressful. Your feline can always be removed from your suite in the event the Landlord's services are required. When an apartment is shared, prior to the purchase or adoption of a feline it is best to first ascertain the legal ownership of the pet. To avoid any complications should the relationship end or the living arrangements change, the ownership of your cat will have been agreed upon in writing and therefore be legally established. Many friendships have been permanently damaged over the love of a cat. As with all possessions and treasured items in your shared home, the ownership of your feline should be finalized before any problems surface.

If you are purchasing a kitten, domestic or purebred, ensure that the paperwork is in the owner's name and as the owner you assume full responsibility for all feline expenses including veterinarian costs. When purchasing a domestic kitten from a pet store or local animal shelter they will issue a receipt stating the legal owner. If you obtain a baby from a home where a litter of domestic kittens have been born it is essential that the veterinarian record of vaccinations and eventual altering clearly state the name of the legal owner.

The Balcony

Apartments and condominiums usually include balconies for the enjoyment of their tenants. However a decision must be made whether that enjoyment should also be extended to your cat. When selecting an apartment it is best to ensure that you have privacy and have solved any possible safety issues if your feline is to be permitted outside balcony access.

When I lived with my cats in a twelve-storey high rise apartment building I had never heard of 'High Rise Syndrome' or HRS. HRS had yet to be acknowledged nor its obvious connection to apartment dwelling felines. Although this condition is presently well documented unfortunately it still occurs with alarming frequency. I believe I was spared this heartbreak through a matter of good fortune and the art of fine feline balance. I realize now that it could easily have happened to any one of my three cats.

Thomas, Dustin's companion cat, loved to sit on the outside ledge of my balcony perched directly above the street, twelve floors away from certain death. He loved the incredible view and the privacy realized on the ledge that was only large enough for his solitary moments of quiet contemplation. I kept my litter boxes on the balcony during the Summer months and therefore could not control his movements while I was away working. When home I would lure him back onto the main balcony with his favorite treats and would then prevent his access to the smaller eight-inch square ledge.

I must stress again that I permitted my cats balcony access before any information was available on the important subject of High Rise Syndrome. It is best to be aware of any situation that could lead to sudden death or danger for your beloved cat. Both the American Humane Association (AHA) and the American Society for the Prevention of Cruelty to Animals (ASPCA) have written extensively on this topic. I wish to acknowledge these sources for the following passages that appear in italics:

High Rise Syndrome

Your apartment is a terrific home for your feline friend. High above the busy streets, your cat will be safe from speeding cars, dangerous diseases and cruel people. However, living in an apartment might not protect your cat from serious injury. Balconies, terraces, fire escapes and open windows can be unseen enemies if you do not take precautions.

While High Rise Syndrome is primarily a problem of city cats, even suburban and country cat owners need to take heed. Although cats usually land on their feet, depending on the distance of the fall and the kind of surface they land on, they can sustain severe injuries and/or death. Cats appear to like perching in dangerous, high places and have little fear of heights. Many owners believe they will not fall. However thousands of them do fall each year from balconies, open windows and rooftops. Sometimes a cat who has been watching a bird will become so focused, he or she may step out into thin air. Likewise, sometimes a cat chasing a moth indoors can sail right out an open unscreened window.

A determined cat can wiggle through the smallest opening of any window or glass sliding door. Tiny balcony ledges are a particular hazard for cats living in high rises. A comfortable body harness and leash held by you is the best protection against any falls.

ASPCA president and CEO Dr. Larry Hawk says, "Pet owners need to know that this syndrome is 100% preventable if they install full window screens and take other simple precautions." When cats fall from high places they don't land squarely on their feet. Instead, they land with their feet slightly splayed apart which can cause severe head and pelvis injuries. It is a misconception that cats won't be injured if they fall from one or two story buildings. They may actually be at greater risk for injury when falling shorter distances than by falling from mid-range or higher altitudes. Shorter distances do not give them enough time to adjust their body posture to fall correctly.

There is a 90% survival rate for cats that are high rise victims if they receive immediate and appropriate medical attention. Cat owners should also make sure they keep their cats indoors to protect them from additional dangers such as cars, other animals, disease or getting lost. People that want to give their cats outdoor stimulation can look into full screen enclosures for backyards and terraces.

If Your Cat Should Fall...

- *Never assume that your cat has been killed, even if you look down and see him/her lying lifeless.*
- *Do not give up looking should your cat disappear after a fall. It is not uncommon for cats to hide in bushes or creep into buildings if the fall has upset or frightened them.*
- *Call your veterinarian immediately.*

Prior to my understanding of HRS I had maintained an open balcony policy and permitted my three cats free liberty. Had I been aware of High Rise Syndrome they would have remained strictly indoors unless I was on the balcony with them. I would have hung planters to prevent any high wire feline acrobatics such as my cats running across the long balcony ledges. I would also have removed all balcony furniture unless I was outside with them. Thomas, my most adventurous wanderer would have been trained to use a cat harness. He never would have discovered the tiny ledge on the outside of my balcony with the spectacular private view which lay before him at free will.

For those residing with enclosed glass screened balconies

your feline is offered the best of both worlds. Your home not only provides additional space, but your cat is given the luxury of fresh air without the dangers outside cats are subjected to on a daily basis. Many condominiums offer completely enclosed balconies that provide felines with a wonderfully fulfilling life. However even those dwelling in apartments are able to extend a limited amount of fresh air to their cats as well. It's not the enclosed outside spaces that are important but rather the love a cat receives and the treasured space they occupy within their owner's heart that truly matters.

~~Time spent with cats is never wasted.~~ May Sarton

Condominium Living

Whether you are renting or have the opportunity to purchase a condo you will be presented with unique and varied challenges. Condo rentals can sometimes be obtained from professionals earning higher incomes who often purchase quality units as yearly tax write-offs. Some professionals will consider their investment as simply a short-term holding property. Others will view their purchase as a longer term retirement investment opportunity. Should you locate the perfect condo consider the age of the professional in determining their true intentions. If you wish a longer term rental it is best to ascertain the owner's commitment of holding the condo as a short or long-term investment. Professionals owning condos are usually concerned with acquiring a responsible tenant to provide income to satisfy annual property taxes and monthly condo fees. Physicians are more inclined to handle their own condo rentals to avoid incurring fees. Conversely, legal professionals desiring their privacy will pay to utilize a rental management company to handle all contact with their tenants.

If you are renting directly from the owner you will have the benefit of additional information prior to committing to a rental agreement. A physician handling their own tenancy requirements will be consumed with maintaining a growing medical practice. They work long hours with their practices requiring time for both business and travel. Many physicians prefer to protect their income and become an incorporated company holding diversified interests. Their condominium concerns will simply be in acquiring a responsible tenant who will care for the property during their many absenses. Once a physician is satisfied they have found a good tenant you may then expect limited contact with the owner. Unless you initiate the contact you may only expect to receive the standard annual rental increases by mail.

Should you be dealing with a rental management company you may have limited information regarding the owner of your suite. If you indicate your preference for a long-term tenancy it is best to not rely on the accuracy of the information provided. The rental management company is only aware of details as provided by their client or the investment company listed as the registered owner of the suite.

The option of renting a condo may be a possibility depending on your area. The deciding factor will be determined by your personal preference and desired length of tenancy. Should the owner wish a yearly lease you may only have the option to rent the suite for that limited period of time. Do not rely on a verbal commitment from an owner despite any confirmation stating they intend to hold the property as a longer term investment. Once the condo has been sold, you will be requested to vacate as more often than not the new owners intend to live in the suite themselves.

Condos may be more costly to rent but will provide a superior living environment. Balconies are often enclosed offering greater privacy and safety for your feline. Sound proofing is usually superior and generally the suites are more spacious. Many condos are provided with personal laundry facilities further eliminating the need to leave the privacy of your suite. Condos are basically self contained units and you will not necessarily experience the same interaction with a Manager or Superintendent as you would in an apartment building. However an appointed Building Committee of condo owners will be present for any problems occurring within the common areas of the building. As you do not own your rental suite you may be spared excessive contact with the Building Committee and will not be required to attend meetings for voting purposes.

Elite and prosperous condominiums may have 24 hour security patrols throughout the building. It is best to be aware that security will be passing your door on a regular basis both night and day. Therefore careful attention should be taken when selecting your Feline by Design as you are seeking the Perfect Condo Kitty for quiet companionship. Please refer to page 56 for our Perfect Condo Kitty Guide.

~~The ideal of calm exists in a sitting cat.~~ Jules Reynard

Townhouses

There are many cat lovers who own their own condo or townhouse but are denied the pleasure of owning a cat. If you are living in a townhouse and can easily enter and exit through your own garage, it becomes easier to keep your feline's presence from the Complex Committee. Also your home is not usually subject to inspection unless there is a major structural problem.

Townhouses are often individually purchased although some complexes are owned by corporations and remain available for rent. If a townhouse is a consideration, your feline may be permitted enclosed balcony access. Townhouses usually consist of two levels and provide adequate space for a feline to explore. Should your townhouse contain an enclosed patio, prior to permitting your cat outside access, consider all safety issues including your cat's visiblity from other suites. When living in a townhouse your cat will have ample space to explore and depending on their activity level should receive adequate exercise. Always supply a scratching pole with sleeping ledges to provide your cat with a private space for rest and observation. You will be encouraging your cat to remain active and such felines seldom scratch furniture when introduced to a quality pole as kittens. Townhouses with two floors totally delight cats as they are drawn to stairs for playful exercise encounters.

If you own your townhouse and your cat is discovered you may be subject to considerable financial fines and penalties. However there is a rarely known clause in many townhouse bylaws that will permit a cat to live within an owner's suite.

One couple interviewed for this publication provided a letter from the wife's physician stating that she had to own a cat due to her emotional instability. With medical documentation the Committee quickly approved the request and permitted the wife to adopt a single cat. The couple had owned their felines for many years but once the Committee approved her request the wife no longer experienced anxiety due to the fear of having her hidden cats discovered. These smart cat lovers had adopted two identically colored cats when originally pur- chasing their townhouse. Although the Committee had only approved the adoption of a single cat she was able to keep them both and no one ever discovered that she in fact cherished two feline treasures.

~~To me, the best holistic remedy for high blood pressure is a purring cat on your lap~~ Kathrine Palmer Peterson

Duplexes and Smaller Homes

My rented home was a duplex with approximately 900 square

feet upstairs and included an unfinished basement of the same size. Although it sounds like a home of adequate size, much of the space was not utilized due to a large staircase which lead from the front door to the living area upstairs or down to the basement. It was an older house with smaller rooms but it remained our home for twenty years and the size did not impede the success of my cattery.

Many rental houses resemble our duplex. Renting such a home is more costly and also carries the responsibility of yard work and maintaining flower beds. However there are additional benefits when not residing close to the property owner. One primary advantage being the reduced stress from concealing your cat's presence. With a semi-detached home such as our duplex you will be sharing a common wall with a neighbor. It is vitally important to keep the peace and maintain a good relationship with all family members. We were blessed to have lived next door to the Curtis family for the entire length of our tenancy. They were aware of my cattery but never disclosed any feline information to our Landlord. I adored Ginger their affectionate and beautiful dog who I always enjoyed caring for while they were away on holidays. It was an ideal situation which does not always occur when duplexes are rented to unrelated families.

If you are considering the rental of a smaller home your cats may be restricted to indoor access only as few smaller houses have balconies or patios. An annual increase in your rent should be a consideration as the Landlord must cope with rising taxes. When residing as a tenant in a house there are also the responsibilities of additional repairs. For many years I was certain my plumbing was held together with yards of duct tape despite the number of repairs by tradesmen. Although the costs can be much higher than residing in an apartment the added benefits are well worth the expense.

Living in Harmony with a Feline

~~Everything a cat is and does physically is to me beautiful, lovely, stimulating, soothing, attractive, and an enchantment.~~ Paul Gallico

If you are hiding your cat in a one-bedroom apartment your feline is adjusting to residing in a smaller space. As they do not have the personal freedom of a cat living in a larger home it is vital to provide a reasonably sized scratching pole. When your cat has a pole that enables them to both climb and sleep on assorted ledges it will serve many functions. Placed near a screened window it will not be seen from outside and your cat will appreciate the height. Your feline will also be provided with an opportunity to exercise as they climb onto the various levels of the pole. If you own a large privacy screen it may be placed near the pole should there be a need to block it's presence in your home. When cats are trained as kittens to use a scratching pole with sleeping ledges, they seldom use their claws inappropriately and rarely scratch furniture. Finally, cat toys should be provided and rotated on a regular basis to prevent boredom.

Provide a greater sense of liberty for your cat by not enforcing excessive rules. While interviewing various tenants hiding their cats it became apparent that those with controlling personalities lay unnecessary limitations on their feline's movements. Rules which are strictly enforced and are contrary to the nature of a feline will often result in negative stress related behavior. Cats living in such an environment may harbor mixed emotions of deep love with those of frustration and anger towards their owner.

In one urgent case I provided an indepth consultation for a couple who owned their pet restricted townhouse. They were hiding a male and female cat and both were declawed as the wife prized her living room furniture. The cats were restricted to a small living space on the main floor and were not permitted upstairs access as the wife equally prized her house plants. The wife had recently purchased expensive leather couches and both cats were forced to endure a second operation to have their back paws declawed as well. Following the second operation the attacks on the wife began.

Prior to the second declawing procedure the male cat had always been loving and affectionate. However now he would routinely attack the wife by biting her arm to the point of drawing blood. The husband was never attacked although it was noted that he never severely disciplined nor restricted the felines' activity within the home. If ever there was a case for banning declawing this was it. This couple was equally ignorant of the additional anxiety they were inflicting upon their cats with the unnecessary space restrictions which further harmed both felines emotionally. The wife appeared unwilling to accept responsibility for her male's aggression despite the problem coinciding with the latest declawing operations. Although it was apparent that the cats were well loved, the male had simply tolerated his boring and stressful environment for too long. He was angry with the wife and he would strike out in the only manner left to him by biting her arm hard enough to draw blood. He too was equally bleeding emotionally and was trying in vain to communicate his discomfort to his beloved owners.

Therefore never create unnecessary anxiety by declawing your cat and do permit him freedom of movement within your home. Permit sitting on tables as felines enjoy heights, and allow those privileges that non cat lovers would never permit and usually frown upon. It is very important to establish and maintain a bond so that you and your cat remain content. When your cat is living in a stress free environment you will not encounter behavioral problems or health issues related to enduring long-term emotional stress.

Another important consideration is to provide the best of everything. The best quality diet will result in fewer visits to your vet. You will then be leaving your apartment with your pet less frequently as your cat will only need a vet check once a year. The best of everything also includes the best quality deodorized clumping cat litter. A high quality deodorized cat litter that clumps is not going to produce offensive odors in your home. With excessive Summer heat bacteria becomes more active and will produce a strong litter box odor that must be avoided. Fewer problems occur in homes where the litter box is cleaned at least twice daily. When a feline is provided with a fresh litter box and the waste materials are removed on a regular basis the air will not be fouled with the scent of soiled litter. If a cat is left with a soiled box they will step on the clumps breaking down the litter which subsequently releases the odor particles into the air. If the box is kept clear the air will also remain clear. Cat lovers residing in a confined space with poor ventilation and not following the above guidelines will find anyone entering their home will know immediately that a feline is in residence.

~~After scolding one's cat, one looks into his face and is seized by the ugly suspicion that he understood every word. And has filed it for reference.~~ Charlotte Gray

Companion Cats

Although some felines are quite comfortable living life as a single cat there are others that prefer company. If you are retired or work from home you may never need to consider a companion cat. However I have always believed felines have the best of both worlds when they are loved by their owners and share their home with a companion. Whether or not your smaller home has pet restrictions you may be presently considering a companion for your beloved feline. In the

Felines by Design chapter we have included a guide of compatible personalities for those who may also wish to own more than one cat and are seeking a kitten.

The amount of time and love you share with your cat can never be replaced by a companion feline. A second cat will provide company permitting you the luxury of additional time away from home for work or outside hobbies. However very little ever replaces an owner's valued presence. Some felines must have a companion cat for their emotional well-being while others are quite content holding reign as the single Queen of their castle. For a short period of time Caterina was my only feline and adjusted well to being the only cat in the house.

The subject of owning multiple cats was discussed with my eight-year-old son Mark once when we were driving. With a serious tone he informed me that once grown he wanted me to live with him, however I would be restricted to staying in his basement. He surprised me as this was one topic we had never discussed before. Although a comfort to be wanted by my child, the thought of living beneath my son's family in a cold basement was not my concept of paradise. I was also amused as I'd never seen Mark so deadly serious before. He then maturely declared that he had one more important stipulation.

Having lived in a cattery for most of his life he was simply tired of cats. He said I was allowed one cat and only one cat. I told him that cats were better in pairs and asked if he would consider permitting me to own a second cat. It was one of those moments in my role as his mother that I've never forgotten. I was touched that he wanted me close by, however I was amused by the expression on his face and the intensity of his manner. I further cautioned him that the family he may one day create with his wife may not appreciate his mother living that near. He didn't appear concerned with his own family but he was deadly serious that I would only be permitted to own just one cat in *his* home.

~~One cat just leads to another~~ Ernest Hemingway

Preparing for Your Feline's Homecoming

~~There are few things in life more heartwarming than to be welcomed by a cat~~ Tay Hohoff

The introduction of a cat into a new home deserves recognition in this book as it focuses on living in harmony with a compatible feline in smaller spaces. I believe there will be readers desiring to enrich their environment with a cat and have never experienced the pleasure a feline brings into their lives. After reading the Felines by Design personalities you may instinctively know which designer kitten will be most suitable living comfortably in your home. Whether you purchase a purebred from a cattery or adopt a domestic from a shelter, every feline is seeking the same instinctive need to love and be loved in return. From lonely adult to active kitten every feline is seeking their owner's loving care and attention. Should you desire to share your heart with a cat, whether you adopt an adult or purchase a kitten you will discover that you have greatly enriched your life.

~~What greater gift than the love of a cat?~~ Charles Dickens

Should you be planning to move into your first apartment never having owned a cat it is imperative to become well informed with this important aspect of feline ownership. It is best to resist the temptation of adopting a stray cat off the street as chances are the cat will simply rebel. A feline not accustomed to living indoors will not reside comfortably in a confined space. It is better to begin by carefully selecting an apartment that will eventually accommodate a feline. Once you are comfortable in your surroundings and have taken the opportunity to observe the building's management, you will be in a better position prior to introducing your cat. After settling into your new home, when adopting the Felines by Design principles you will enjoy greater success in selecting the right kitten.

As you are living in a smaller space greater care is needed prior to your cat's homecoming. The highest quality and age appropriate diet for your feline should be provided at all times. It is best to place your feline's fresh water beside her food and to change the water twice daily. The breed and size of your cat should also be considered when providing bowls of adequate size. For example, Persian and Himalayan cats have extreme faces and require wide bowls well filled to enable them to comfortably eat and drink.

An adequately sized open litter box with superior quality clumping litter and a wide slotted litter spoon for waste removal are essential. The placement of the litter box is important as your cat will be trained to the specific area chosen. It is essential to promote good feline hygiene by cleaning the litter box at least twice daily even when only a single kitten is in residence. More problems surface from litter box neglect than any other in my consultation practice. Although there is always an exception to the rule a feline that is accustomed to a clean box seldoms displays behavioral problems such as random wetting. Additionally, a scratching pole with sleeping ledges is essential for both exercise and a kitten's emotional security. The added bonus is that a kitten provided with a scratching pole will rarely climb curtains or scratch furniture.

It is important to ensure your feline's continued safety by removing all toxic plants in your home. Placing them out of reach is simply not good enough and it is best to just give them away. The vast list of toxic plants is continuously expanding. Your veterinarian is best to advise which plants are safe and may provide current literature to enable a safer homecoming. Some felines, especially kittens, are attracted to dangling wires and plugs. Therefore whenever possible such areas should be covered or hidden. With an assortment of toys that are rotated to prevent boredom, your feline is less likely to be attracted to an unsafe area. If wire chewing becomes a problem it can be discouraged with the use of a cat repellent. Your veterinarian is aware of the better products available and should be consulted before making any purchase.

Bringing Baby Home

It is best to introduce your feline, whether adult or kitten, to their new home as early in the morning as possible. When a feline is given a full day to adjust to their new surroundings they are less likely to become stressed and cry during their first evening home. As they will be residing in a smaller space this advantage will provide your cat with an opportunity to become quickly acquainted with their surroundings.

Introduce your new baby to her home by leaving the kitten in her carrier with the door open directly beside her freshly filled litter box. Some felines will quickly leave the security of their carriers while others may take a longer period to adjust to the unfamiliar scents and sounds within their new home. Your kitten should be permitted time to both adjust and explore her new environment without your interaction. Adult cats may slink along the walls and then remain hidden under a couch or bed. While she remains hidden speak to her and call her by name and eventually she will make her entrance anxious to socialize. She will eventually become curious and comfortable to both explore her home and make acquaintance with her owner.

Before bringing your feline home it is essential to have arranged at least ten days off from work. This is necessary to provide your kitten the time to bond with you and quietly adjust to her new environment. You are less likely to encounter behavioral problems or a lonely frightened kitten crying for company while you are not home. While enjoying time with your kitten try periods of training by leaving her alone and listening outside your door to know what to expect in the future. Once back at work, when possible use your lunch break for a quick trip home to ensure your kitten is adapting well during your absence. Some kittens become comfortable with their owner's absence while others require a gradual period of adjustment to being left alone.

Those cat lovers that have adopted an adult feline will reap the rewards once returning to work as adults appear more comfortable when left alone at home. The age of your kitten and her designer personality will eventually determine the liberty you will be comfortable providing to her. Every home has a rythym of it's own. If you have taken as much time as possible with your kitten you will be aware of her energy levels, sleeping patterns and will have prepared for her bouts of activity during your absence. Leave a radio playing low while your feline is left alone. This will serve two purposes: company for your kitten and a sound buffer for anyone passing your door.

Prior to your kitten settling into her new environment be aware of areas where she might eventually become enclosed. If your suite has a washer and dryer always check without fail with each load of laundry dried that your kitten or cat has not claimed the dryer as a warm resting place. Before adding wet clothes and after removing dried clothes from your dryer, always check your appliance before closing the dryer door and leaving the laundry area. Felines move quickly and can jump into a dryer in the blink of an eye. They will use the few seconds needed to place dry clothes on a table for folding to explore a certain death trap. The bathroom may also become an unnecessary hazzard. However if toilet seat covers are always left down and a bathtub filled with water is never left unattended your kitten will remain safe.

Kittens love sleeping near their owner however much

depends on the preference of both owner and personality of the designer feline. The Sophisticated Feral designer personality is often a loner. These felines may initially prefer sleeping in the same room but at a comfortable distance from their owner. Kittens are accustomed to the warmth of litter mates and therefore many kittens prefer to be as close as possible to their caregiver. Caterina slept across my neck her first week at home. We simply needed each other and those nights proved beneficial and developed into a loving and permanent bond in our relationship.

~~Only cat lovers know the luxury of fur-coated, musical hot water bottles that never go cold.~~ Susanne Millen

Due to the depth and complexity of the various feline personalities Volumes 2 and 3 in the Felines by Design series[1] will examine this subject in greater detail. The size of the home and new family, the age of the kitten or adult feline are all individually addressed. Some felines may be entering a multi-cat home, while others may be an addition completing their feline family as a companion kitten to a senior cat. There is much to be understood from the introduction of a single young kitten with one owner residing in a smaller space to the adoption of an adult feline into a larger multi-cat home. Every situation and every feline is unique, but when proper protocol is followed the bonding within various situations are usually met with success.

There is a massive quantity of information available on this important area of interest. Writers, breeders, vets and assorted web sites offer broad and sometimes conflicting advice. I have endeavoured to cover only the basics in welcoming a feline into their new home. My personal concept is that I greatly respect every kitten born as possessing a unique and loving

[1] Felines by Design series: Volume 2: Insider's Guide to Buying Purebred Kittens, Volume 3: Insider's Guide to Selecting Domestic Felines

soul. Therefore above all else I prefer to honor the individual bonding process that gradually develops between a feline and their loving caregiver. When your kitten becomes a part of your household she is truly blessing your home. Regarding the loving care of a kitten, always follow your own common sense. When nurturing a bond with your feline, I believe it is best to follow those loving instincts as dictated by your heart.

~~Cats are absolute individuals with their own ideas about everything, including the people they own~~ John Dingman

Proper Litter Box Etiquette

Before bringing your feline home decide in advance where you wish the litter box to be placed in your apartment. Kittens may display an aversion to change once they have been trained to a specific area. Therefore anticipate your needs to ensure you will not be required to change the placement of their box. A superior quality clumping litter in an adequately sized open box is best. Refrain from purchasing an expensive covered litter box where the feline is required to enter and exit through a small opening. Although well ventilated and providing privacy such enclosed covered litter boxes have been known to cause internal problems with larger felines. The constant crouching in a confined space may actually shorten your cat's life span. An open box is best, a good quality clumping litter mandatory and adopting a routine of removing waste from your cat's litter box twice daily is absolutely essential.

As a Feline Behavior Consultant many of my consultations are regarding the cat's inappropriate use of their litter box. A feline must initially be vet checked to determine that there are no medical issues present which may be causing the cat's behavior. After a veterinarian has certified the feline is in good health the problem is often referred to me. In order to understand the situation clearly I begin working with the owner to ascertain the message of discomfort which their feline is attempting to communicate. When a problem exists within a home quite often a cat will use their litter box as their only manner to communicate their high levels of stress and frustration.

It has been my experience that even the most loving and attentive owners will neglect their cat's litter box on a semi-regular basis. Although the owner may refuse to use an unsanitary public washroom they somehow fail to appreciate their feline's similar disgust with the sight and scent from a dirty litter box. Even feline specialists have consulted with me on this most important subject. Many times the very life of the cat lies in the balance in discovering the reason for random litter box use with a cat that at one time was always clean. During such consultations I always ask a series of questions reserving the final question of how often the litter box is being cleaned on a daily basis. I have discovered even professional cat lovers must confess to bouts of litter box neglect due to their feline's facility being kept in an inconspicuous area within their home.

The misconception behind felines and the inappropriate use of their litter box have involved so many consultations that I could write a volume on this one subject alone. I have attended countless in-home consultations and written online articles regarding the inappropriate etiquette of a feline with her litter box. In my experience many times the problem results from a client neglecting to clean their feline's litter on a regular basis. Whether you are fortunate enough to own five cats or have a personal relationship with only one feline it is mandatory to clean their box at least twice a day. If it becomes a ritual where your cat's box is cleaned before leaving for work in the morning and before you sit down after coming home in the evening you will save yourself not only additional work but possible heartache as well.

There are situations in life where a little work now saves us greater problems in the future. I am not mechanically minded but I know the importance of regular oil changes for my car. Mothers who have been diligent with changing their baby's diapers on a regular basis will usually reap their rewards when toilet training time arrives. A child who is accustomed to feeling clean is easier to train as their personal cleanliness has developed into a comfortable habit. Hence it is best to begin with healthy hygiene in a cat's most personal area of self-expression. Chances are you will never have a feline trying to communicate their discomfort with your lack of attention to their litter box. This is an easy solution to a costly problem that appears obvious in it's simplicity but more often than not is overlooked.

For many owners when their cat's litter box is placed out of sight it also becomes an issue of being out of mind. This often leads to absent minded neglect until their cat protests by leaving random stool samples or wetting directly beside their dirty box. This is a sure sign that the owner has neglected this critical aspect of their feline's most personal area of care. Cats are respectfully territorial. When you display respect and regularly clean their litter box they will return the compliment and be respectfully clean within the personal space of your home.

~~If you would know what a cat is thinking about, you must hold his paw in your hand for a long time...~~
Jules Champfleury

Travelling with Your Cat

~~Cats are connoisseurs of comfort~~ James Herriot

There are a vast assortment of pet carriers available that can be used to safely transport a feline. If you have an accommodating and comfortable handbag you can safely transport your cat from your apartment directly to the car. A folding cloth pet carrier can be purchased and stored in your vehicle until it is required. Prior to bringing your cat to the car have the carrier ready in the back seat secured in place using a seat belt. It is much easier to have your vehicle packed with everything in place prior to bringing your feline to the car.

Although many cats are able to comfortably enjoy a short two or three hour drive, some felines have smaller bladders. Therefore when in doubt purchase absorbant liners through your local medical supply outlet. Placing the absorbant liners in the carrier will keep your cat comfortable as she will remain clean and dry. Jewel, my Blue Point Himalayan, once required surgery which necessitated a lengthy 4 hour trip to her Specialist in Washington State. Jewel required frequent restroom breaks and her liners were changed several times during the trip. The liners are a wonderful asset when travelling with cats as they not only absorb urine and keep your cat dry, but they also do not release any odor.

If you plan to take your cat on vacation, San Francisco SPCA's President Daniel Crain offers tips to keep pets safe during the Summer months as well as when travelling. I wish to acknowledge this source as well as the Humane Society of the United States (HSUS) for the following passages that appear in italics:

• *Never leave pets in a parked vehicle. Temperatures*

inside cars can rise to 120 degrees Fahrenheit in just a few minutes. If pets aren't allowed inside with their owners leave them at home on hot days.

- *Prevent dehydration.* Keep animals refreshed with non-tip water bowls. Bowls should be kept full of fresh water at home. When travelling, carry a container of fresh water or some ice cubes.

- *Keep pets inside.* Don't leave pets outside unsupervised on hot days. If pets are outside, make sure they have access to plenty of fresh water and shade (but remember that shade moves as the sun moves.)

- *Don't drive with pets in the back of a pick-up truck.* Cats should ride in the cab in a secured carrier. Acclimate cats to the car with short car rides, and keep them in a carrier at all times.

- *Pack important pet travel necessities.* Pack toys, bedding, litter box, cleaning supplies, a first aid kit, medical records, any medications that your pets need and the phone number of their veterinarian.

- *Microchip pets.* Tiny microships programmed with an identification number can be implanted under the skin between a pet's shoulder blades. If a lost pet turns up in a shelter, the chip can be scanned and checked against a central registry to locate the owner.

- *In addition,* pets should wear suitable appropriately sized collars with identification tags indicating the owner's permanent address and a phone number where they can be reached during a trip. In addition, always carry a current photo of your pets in case posters and flyers need to be made.

If you decide to take your cat on vacation, start planning your trip early. You will need to research places that provide pet friendly accommodations, determine if your cat will need a health certificate and schedule a pre-vacation veterinary exam.

HOW TO HIDE YOUR CAT FROM THE LANDLORD

You will want to make sure that you carry proof of a current rabies vaccination.

Travelling by Plane

The HSUS recommends that cats be transported by air only if absolutely necessary. Air travel poses special risks for all pets. According to the Air Traffic Association, more than 5,000 animals are killed, injured or lost on commercial flights each year. Most injuries and deaths to animals travelling by airplane are due to extreme heat or cold, poorly ventilated cargo holds, mishandling by baggage personnel, and damage to carriers. If you must travel by air with your pet, keep the following in mind.

- *Not all airlines will carry pets. Call the airline well in advance of your trip to make sure that they accept pets and to check health and immunization requirements for your cat.*
- *Take cats on board with you in carriers that fit under the seat.*
- *Contact airlines for specific requirements, including type and size of carrier, for taking your cat on board.*
- *Take direct flights to avoid mistakes and delays that occur with transfers and schedule flights early or late in the day to avoid extreme heat.*
- *If you cannot take your cat on board with you in a carrier, then notify the captain and at least one flight attendant that your cat is travelling in the cargo hold. If the captain knows there are pets on board he or she may take special precautions.*
- *Fit your cat with a collar that can't get caught in carrier doors. Instead of a dangling tag, affix identification on the collar and carrier with your name, address and phone number, as well as a temporary travel ID with the address and phone number where*

you can be reached at your travel destination.

Travelling by Ship or Train
- *Most cruise lines don't accept pets with the exception of assistance dogs.*
- *Amtrak currently does not accept pets for transport unless they are assistance dogs. There may be smaller U.S. rail companies that permit animals on board their trains. Many trains in Europe allow pets.*
- *Many restaurants and tourist attractions do not allow pets. If you're not prepared to go the extra mile to accommodate your pet during travel, he or she may be safer and happier at home.*
- *Research the pet sitting services in your area.*

There are many varieties of oversized handbags available to transport your feline in and out of your home. My Caterina loved her cozy "hotel" handbag which she associated with travel and adventure. When I went on trips I had my credit card readily available for the hotel desk clerk and still kept Caterina silent. I always had one hand in the bag stroking her while I was registering and signing my name. Despite Caterina's distinctly loud Himalayan voice she always remained quiet within her bag. She was a feline that craved adventure. I always believed that she instinctively knew she was involved in an environment of suspense and her silence was an important part of the scenario. Although it is necessary to have a cat with the temperament of my beloved Caterina if you must travel for business a Sociable Independant is always ready for an adventure.

After checking into your room spend a few minutes with your cat while she explores the suite. Leave the television set on prior to leaving the room and returning to your car. It is best to transport your luggage through the lobby when returning to your hotel suite. However, when you return to your vehicle for feline supplies carry everything concealed within a black garbage bag into your hotel room using the back entrance.

Caterina and I were well prepared the next morning before our room was to be cleaned. All evidence of her presence in the room would be concealed prior to housekeeping staff gaining entry. I would lift her food and water dishes and put them in a grocery bag safely hidden within a drawer. Her litter box would be enclosed in a garbage bag and placed on the upper shelf of the closet or safely locked in my empty suitcase prior to leaving the room. When vacationing with your cat it is best to always be prepared and my investment in a compact litter box, especially suited for car travel was very convenient. I always brought numerous empty grocery bags with me to dispose of litter box evidence and all other trash in the hotel room.

Early in the morning I would inquire when housekeeping was expected to clean my room. Once I was aware of the time sequence involved, I knew the correct method to use when concealing my cat's presence. We usually stayed together in the car when it was only a matter of 20 minutes before our room was ready. Therefore Caterina only experienced a short wait in her carrier before she was back in our room. I was always concerned with providing proper ventilation and only with temperature permitting would Caterina be placed in her car carrier until our room had been cleaned by the housekeeping staff. If I was in any doubt of her comfort level Caterina and I would spend a few hours in air conditioned luxury driving through the tourist areas of town until the staff had prepared our suite. If the housekeeping schedule was later than met my needs, the room was cleaned while Caterina and I both attended my business meetings in the early afternoon.

Many hotels will provide accommodation for cats but some will request a small cover charge for a pet. However whether or not Caterina was a registered guest I always made sure she remained with me and in her carrier while the room was being cleaned. It was safer and the staff did not have to be concerned with her wandering the halls and possibly becoming lost. If I was away in a meeting I didn't have to worry about her. We both preferred our privacy and enjoyed the evenings together. She loved the entire experience and I didn't have to worry about her being lonely at home.

Felines by Design

The Cat Lover's Manual for
Selecting the Perfect Condo Kitty

The Felines by Design principles are a great asset in showcasing specific personality types when looking to compliment an owner's preferences and lifestyle. Whether you seek a domestic or purebred kitten you will have the knowledge to locate what we affectionately refer to as the Perfect Condo Kitty. A Perfect Condo Kitty is a kitten that thrives in apartment life and whose personality will have the greatest potential to flourish within a smaller home.

When actively searching for a feline, an owner is hoping to find an affectionate personality that will bond with them and become an important part of their lives. Possessing the ability to successfully match a kitten's personality with their owner is a skill good breeders are keen to develop. It is my desire that should you be seeking a compatible kitten our guidelines will enlighten you beyond even a breeder's abilities in selecting the right kitten.

Following years of breeding and selling kittens, my focus became centered on the compatibility of matching the right kitten with each buyer. After a litter is born the various personalities emerge as the babies mature. Every kitten is different displaying individual preferences for handling and affection. When the compatible designer feline is matched with the appropriate owner the bonding becomes intensely complete.

Those living in an apartment are seeking a feline that is both compatible and will be comfortable residing in a smaller home. Volumes 2 and 3 in the Felines by Design series[2] provide detailed information that greatly assists buyers looking to select a perfect and compatible kitten. The following excerpts are taken from these publications and are presented in abridged form. The Felines by Design principles are not breed specific and apply equally to both purebred and domestic felines. When a cat has been selected using the Felines by Design principles a buyer has a greater chance of locating their Feline Soul Mate.

The following personalities are being presented as those designer felines who are more comfortable residing with a loving owner in smaller spaces. Our information will assist you in selecting your own Perfect Condo Kitty from the many litters available in your area. Additionally, if you already own a cat you may wish to review the following personalities to discover hidden jewels of knowledge about your own treasured feline.

~~As anyone who has ever been around a cat for any length of time well knows, cats have enormous patience with the limitations of the human mind.~~ Cleveland Amory

[2] Felines by Design series: Volume 2: Insider's Guide to Buying Purebred Kittens, Volume 3: Insider's Guide to Selecting Domestic Felines

- 55 -

Personality	Sex	Good for 1st Cat Owner	Good with Children	Will Accept New Spouse	Travels Well	Accepts Other Cats	Compatibility
Dignified A Gentleman	M	Yes	Yes	Yes	Yes^2	Yes	With all except H
Lady of B Distinction	F	Yes	Yes^1	Yes	Yes^2	Yes	With all except H
Sociable C Independent	M/F	Yes	Yes	Yes	Yes^3	Yes	Female accepts all; Male not H
Peter D Pan	M	Yes	Yes	Yes	Depends	Yes	With all except H
Precious E Treasure	F	Yes	Depends	Yes	No	Yes	With all except G & H
Sophisticated F Feral	M/F	No	No	Depends	No	Yes	With all except H
Bewitching G Goddess	F	Yes	Yes	Yes	Yes^3	Yes	With all except E & H
Feline H Zeus	M	No	No	No	No	Depends	Sometimes with Female C
Lovable I Teddy Bear	M	Yes	Depends	Yes	Yes^2	Yes	With all except H
Devoted J Spirit	F	Yes	No	Yes	Yes^3	Yes	With all except H
Feline K Chameleon	M/F	Yes	No	Depends	Depends	Depends	With all except H

Table 1.0 - Felines by Design: Perfect Condo Kitty Personality Guide

Note: 1: Good with older respectful children only. 2: Short day trips by car only. 3: Can also adapt to air travel

Dignified Gentleman

~~It is in their eyes that their magic resides.~~ Arthur Symons

If you are looking for the perfect balance of both independence and loving feline interaction this easy care kitten may be perfect for you. Although these intriguing and endearing males are few and far between when provided with the right information you will learn to recognize them. Such kittens appear to already possess an instinctive understanding of their place within the world. Upon owning a Dignified Gentleman when looking into their eyes you will see to the depths of their souls.

I had the pleasure of owning one stud male who was the epitome of the Dignified Gentleman. Spencer was so endearing had I the power to transform him into a human he would have been the perfect man. It may seem a ridiculous thought but in retrospect he was simply enchanting. Perhaps only another breeder could comprehend how endearing the relationship with her stud male can be. It was my unexpressed wish to have owned him as my only cat. However that honor was bestowed upon a close friend when he was eventually petted out. Over the years several of Spencer's litters produced Dignified Gentlemen. As these were unique and personable babies I was selective when placing them. Such felines make extraordinary companions and the waiting list for Spencer's special kittens was always long.

For a cat breeder, the Dignified Gentleman is easy to identify as a kitten. Depending on the dynamics of the litter they comfortably ease into the role of leader. Born with a highly perceptive intelligence, yet possessing a gentle manner this is the baby that will always be noticed. As with all healthy kittens he actively plays with litter mates and displays a natural curiosity of the world around him. However when in the cattery this kitten is only truly content when interacting with the loving person who has handled him since birth. Often leaving his litter mates and mother in the nursery he will seek his beloved breeder's attention preferring to spend quality time in her company. He becomes difficult to resist and while in the cattery this darling male will become his breeder's choice as her favorite kitten.

The Dignified Gentleman at four weeks of age will desire a longer period of cuddling than his brothers and sisters. This male often follows his mother into the litter box and will instinctively use it apparently understanding its intended purpose. He will then lead his litter mates to further explore his latest discovery for an extended play session in the sandy textured substance. Following several days of such play his brothers and sisters will also be litter box trained. I was delighted when spared this time consuming task by those special males born in the nursery. Every breeder fondly remembers her precious Feline by Design kittens that were born as Dignified Gentlemen in the cattery.

This unique designer kitten is a pleasure to raise. They follow the standard six to eight week growth pattern by developing their sense of independence through exploration and play. At this stage of development this male no longer desires to be handled as often. However one subtle difference is that he will routinely seek the comforting presence of his beloved breeder for extended periods of cuddling. This is uncommon during the active age of six to eight weeks as kittens are mobile and usually prefer exploring the cattery.

Due to his higher than normal intelligence this male possesses a longer memory than most felines. These cats are uncanny in their recollection of those who have loved or mistreated them with any unkindness. As spiritual felines they are aware when their owner returns home tired after a difficult day's work. During depressing or stressful periods of time he will instinctively appear desiring to provide comforting support. This male will shadow your every move until he is satisfied your discomfort has passed.

These extremely sensitive cats will become agitated with any changes occurring within their environment. The re-positioning of furniture or mirrors within rooms will greatly disturb them. A loving owner will return the mirror to its original wall or move any furniture back into place in order to pacify their sweet natured male. The Dignified Gentleman will then display great appreciation for such kindness bestowed upon them. This particular Feline by Design prefers routine and the security found only within his home. The liberty that is provided to an outside cat would be overwhelming and simply unsuitable for him. Without having to establish an outside territory he takes great comfort in guarding his home and loved ones.

The Dignified Gentleman is the feline that remains by their owner's side during illness never leaving the bedroom. This male becomes instinctively aware of an impending emergency or when his owner should be awakened during a crisis. I have personally owned one such male, a domestic tabby I named Dustin. As a young woman he awoke me during the evening on two separate occasions. Once when my home was going to be robbed and the other when his companion cat Thomas was in serious trouble and would have died without my assistance. Take notice when owning one of these males especially should they display behavior which is completely out of character. Normally a content and quiet male he will use advanced vocalizing and will become extremely agitated attempting to communicate the danger he is anticipating.

They have a manner unlike any other Feline by Design male. They take the greatest pleasure in greeting you in the evening when you return home from work. He is a Perfect Condo Kitty because he delights in quietly exploring his world and is content and comfortable in smaller homes. He does well in a family environment, with a senior or as a single cat simply loving one owner. He is always a pleasure to own and will even accept the addition of a spouse should his owner decide to marry. Single women or those divorced and living alone find this male a particularly comforting presence.

Prior to becoming a breeder I was living alone in a condominium with my cat Dustin. This wonderful male, my first kitten, nutured a life long interest of working and understanding the mystique and behavior of cats. Totally inexperienced with felines I was unprepared one evening when he initially displayed an uncanny ability to protect me.

Over the years having owned him since he was five-weeks-old it became his preference to sleep on my bed. However this familiar routine changed one evening over a long holiday weekend. Despite several attempts to coax him to bed he absolutely refused to enter the room. Loudly vocalizing his concern Dustin began to actively prowl every room in the condo. Following additional unsuccessful attempts to pacify him I eventually closed the bedroom door to sleep. Within the first half hour he began to repetitively throw his body against my closed bedroom door. After opening the door several times he absolutely refused to enter. Instead he returned to the living room to continue his odd feline wailing as though he was in danger.

Typical of the Dignified Gentleman, Dustin was always a quiet and reserved male. His behavior became so bizarre following several repeated episodes I left the bedroom turning on every light in the condominium. I also turned on the stereo trying to soothe him and wondered if possibly an earthquake was imminent. Once I left the bedroom he continued vocalizing for another ten minutes. Within the hour Dustin appeared satisfied and decided it was now time to sleep. His mistress was awake and therefore his task had been successfully completed. My night was ruined and unable to rest I remained awake until dawn.

On the final afternoon of that Labor Day weekend the police informed me that every condo on my floor had been robbed.

Those suites surrounding my own were vacant while my neighbors took advantage of the final long weekend of Summer. Immediately I understood why Dustin had been so disturbed the evening before. I still wonder had I not remained awake playing my music until dawn would something have happened to me that night. Robbery is always an unsettling and dangerous situation. However Dustin saved us from what would have been a home invasion and prevented further personal injury which may have occurred. He was my feline hero and the very first of those few Dignified Gentlemen I would love, eventually breed and be so blessed to own.

If you are fortunate to find a Dignified Gentleman as a kitten or adult feline your life will be enriched by his loving presence. These Felines by Design are remembered, cherished and due to their endearing personalities usually find their human soul mates in their lifetime.

~~Cats are the eye of God~~ T lobsang Rampa

Lady of Distinction

~~Loneliness is comforted by the closeness and touch of fur to fur, skin to skin, or skin to fur~~ Paul Gallico

In a cattery many litters are born and subsequently sold. The dedicated breeder remains in constant motion anxiously tending to the needs of her many litters and breeding felines. A breeder handles her kittens daily providing quality loving care and attention. Gentle interaction with young babies is necessary to promote an affectionate nature in the emerging personalities of the kittens. As the years pass individual babies are sometimes difficult to recall. However, occasionally a kitten is born with qualities so unique her memory leaves an indelible imprint upon her breeder's heart. This gentle Feline by Design kitten is known as the Lady of Distinction. She is the darling female that perfectly mirrors the unique qualities of the Dignified Gentleman. This is the baby the breeder will sell with deep regret as she truly wanted to keep the kitten for herself.

As a young kitten she seems so wise it appears that she has been here before. She simply understands the routine and bonds quickly with her breeder as there is a natural flow of affection between them. The Lady of Distinction will elect to be cuddled and held rather than seek adventure in wandering the nursery. She appears to be above playing with litter mates apparently unable to comprehend their pleasure in rough and tumble play. An unusually gentle kitten she prefers to watch their antics from her breeder's lap simply amused by the action taking place on the floor below. This kitten may seem out of place as she appears to have a more worldly perception of her surroundings and loves her breeder before everything else.

At six weeks of age this baby's place is always above her litter mates in a position of observation. The Lady of Distinction will prefer sleeping on the sofa or ideally her breeder's lap. Wise beyond her years this sweetheart tugs at your heartstrings. Breeders are always torn when the decision must be made to sell one of these unique designer kittens. As women we try to convince ourselves that no one could possibly ever love or understand this kitten as much as we do. However as professional breeders, in order to keep our cattery small and manageable we simply are not permitted the luxury of following our hearts. While she is ours we cherish our time with this baby and are extremely selective when finding the right home for her.

This dynamic baby not only prefers to be held but also mirrors other qualities of the Dignified Gentleman. When you love this adorable and wise kitten looking into her eyes you will also see her tender soul. Unlike other kittens she is able to communicate all her needs with one simple glance at her breeder. This one truly separates herself from the other kittens in the cattery. However due to her quiet and non-demanding nature only those captivated by her mystique are able to comprehend the depth of this rare beauty.

This kitten is the feline of style and character, truly a classic beauty irresistible to those able to recognize her depth of soul. The memory of this one remains with her beloved breeder. She is the Feline by Design each breeder will regretfully sell knowing how deeply her presence will be missed. She will long be remembered as the kitten they should have kept.

The Lady of Distinction is a Perfect Condo Kitty adaptable to every living situation. She accepts smaller homes provided that there are higher areas made available as places for quiet observation. A quality scratching pole with sleeping ledges placed near a window will keep her satisfied during her owner's absence. She also enjoys a social environment and will readily welcome visitors into her home. This feline is best suited for an owner who prefers weekends and evenings at home as the importance of her caregiver's presence is necessary to keep her content. If her owner should marry, this feline will adapt well to change as long as she is able to love and share time with each family member.

To truly understand the Lady of Distinction it should be understood that this darling has long been separated from the species of feline. She is a lady that you simply never forget. Born above title of cat, this lovely girl is not a snob nor will she show the playful agressiveness of the Sociable Independent. She simply knows her place and acts accordingly. She is not difficult to please as long as she remains comfortable within her loving family. When you have been blessed with her presence in your life you are able to understand why this enchanting girl seems to be more than a cat. Over time she is equal to a long intimate relationship with a beloved friend. Both selected clients and friends wanted to own these exceptional kittens. It was understood that they would be placed on a waiting list, as these special kittens were not produced in every litter. When such a female was born in my cattery it was extremely difficult for me to part with them. Therefore it became mandatory when placing these incredible females that I was well acquainted with the home and family.

This kitten is born in both domestic and purebred litters. If you are searching for this exceptional Feline by Design kitten take note of her qualities and closely question the breeder regarding her personality. These lovely kittens born with such irresistible charm are treasured and usually spend their entire lifetime with one owner. The Lady of Distinction is totally devoted to her family and has little difficulty in locating her human soul mate. When she becomes a part of your life simply to know her is to love and treasure her.

~~If we treated everyone we meet with the same affection we bestow upon our favorite cat, they, too, would purr.~~
Martin Buxbaum

Sociable Independent

~~When you come upon your cat, deep in meditation, staring thoughtfully at something that you can't see, just remember that your cat is, in fact, running the universe.~~
Bonni Elizabeth Hall and Missycat

This totally adorable and sociable Feline by Design personality is treasured by their families. This cat maintains the perfect balance of devotion for their family while meeting their personal need for restful periods of solitude. Although there are subtle differences between the male and female Sociable Independent they are always loving and active felines in their homes.

True to their Feline by Design title, the Sociable Independent is the official greeter for all visitors. Guests are warmly welcomed and entertained by this feline until their owner is able to adequately center her attention on their company. This independent sweetheart will then retreat nearby in restful solitude to quietly observe their guests.

Female Sociable Independent

~~Most of us rather like our cats to have a streak of wickedness. I should not feel quite easy in the company of any cat that walked about the house with a saintly expression~~
Beverly Nichols

The female Sociable Independent exhibits a strong maternal instinct coupled with stubborn resistance. She loves and mothers all those she accepts as family. This feline is one of the few designer personalities to quickly accept other pets into her treasured space. She routinely cleans her companion cats and also closely monitors and mothers her beloved owner and other family members. This female loves attention and posing for pictures. She is the only movie star of the Feline by Design personalities with a strong preference to be included in all family videos and photos.

As she ages this cat develops into an intellectual sponge and may possess the ability to read her owner's thoughts. My Sociable Independent will anticipate the exact time I will require her presence prior to leaving for her veterinarian appointment. She will simply disappear and not until the vet's office has closed for the day will she make her whereabouts known.

The Sociable Independent is a wonderful companion and will be totally comfortable in her role as the Perfect Condo Kitty. She balances her treasured time of independent solitude equally with seeking her owner's company as an affectionate lap cat. This personality blends well with a couple or a single owner residing in an apartment or larger home. She thrives in either a busy household or in the quiet home of a retired senior. She can also adapt well to living with respectful children and is stimulated by company and changes within her accepted routine.

This personality follows her own heart and will be stubborn once comfortable with her personal decisions. It will be difficult to sway her from sleeping on freshly cleaned linen should your laundry area be her sleeping place of choice. It is far easier to remove the laundry than to remove her. She is stubbornly resistant to change once a pattern has been established within her personal routine.

This feline is a companion in the truest sense of the word. As a lap cat she leaves no uncertainty as to where her loyalties lie. She truly is a lover of home and family. This feline believes in sharing her devotion and will charm each member of her family by alternately selecting them as her chosen favorite. However after a period of time she will quickly change direction and abandon her chosen favorite's lap. She will then transfer her love and total devotion to another family member by only accepting their lap in the evening. One should never take offense by her whims as this feline only appears fickle. She simply believes in equally distributing her affections which will become rather apparent when she resides with a couple.

The female Sociable Independent loves her treats and takes all food quite seriously. Samples from her owner's dinner may simply be considered an extension of her personal dining pleasure. However this is not a Cupboard Loving Kitty. Her devotion to her owner is sincere and not always dictated by her stomach.

Everyone from family to guest loves the Sociable Independent. Visitors warmly remember this feline as she presents a totally welcoming persona in her home. She will gravitate towards change and thrives on activity. Apartment life is satisfying to her especially when her family takes time in their busy schedules to always include her. When residing with more than a single owner she becomes well acquainted with all family schedules. This lovely feline enjoys being surrounded by company but prefers when each family member maintains a familiar routine. Depending on her mood she may decide to play the role of the sleeping office cat or will make her presence known by demanding attention. As this feline thrives on change she travels well and is a perfect Hotel Kitty should her owner travel for business or pleasure. For tips on travelling with your cat please refer to page 48.

~~When I play with my cat, how do I know that she is not passing time with me rather than I with her?~~ Montaigne

Male Sociable Independent

~~Your cat will never threaten your popularity by barking at three in the morning. He won't attack the mailman or eat the drapes, although he may climb the drapes to see how the room looks from the ceiling~~ Helen Powers

This designer personality surfaces both in catteries of registered purebreds and domestic litters of varied coloring. However, it is more commonly found in the genetic coloring within domestic litters of lovely orange tabby kittens. Although I have never had the pleasure of owning an orange tabby, over the years I have been befriended by several of these special boys. Those domestic tabbys that have permitted me to become a part of their lives represent the classic example of the male Sociable Independent.

Purebred male and female kittens of this designer personality are endearing and always sell quickly. These kittens initially enjoy being held by their breeder but will appropriately distance themselves when they are six to eight-weeks-old. They are sociable kittens but exploration, play and eating remain their primary focus during this stage of their development. If you are interested in a domestic litter you may discover the male tabby will display a greater interest in being handled at this age than the purebred tabby.

The Sociable Independent's true nature will become more evident after leaving the cattery and settling into their new home.   Without the stimulation of litter mates and security found in their breeder's company they quickly bond with their new family. To have a kitten with this designer personality is a wonderful experience. They are comical but demanding felines with a loving devotion for both home and family. They are blessed with an extensive personality and believe the world has been created just for their personal amusement.

This feline believes in living life to the fullest. The male tabbys I have encountered were outside cats and well known in the neighborhood as they endeavored to explore and discover every nook and cranny. If you have ever opened your back door to a feline waiting for a friendly interlude, chances are you've encountered this engaging sweetheart. Unlike the female Sociable Independent with a love for food he is not quite the same Cupboard Loving Kitty. This male is not expecting a hand out but rather an appreciation of his effortless charms. A few kind words, perhaps a snack or two and he is off on his rounds anxious to greet the next neighbor he has befriended.

Many times during our interviews those owners blessed with such a lovable male have echoed similar sentiments. This designer personality lives to love his owner and is always anxious to befriend anyone he encounters along the way. Provided he is honored as head cat he may even accept other outside cats dwelling within his neighboring territory. This male's quest not only extends to befriending his neighbors but will include the paper carrier, the postal carrier and milkman who will all stop to acknowledge this sweet boy.

If this male has decided you have harmed him in any way he will snub you for the remainder of his life. During our interviews we were told of one Sociable Independent who was the altered ginger tom of the neighborhood. While still a kitten his owner had decided that while she worked during the day he was to remain outside. As an affectionate male always seek-ing companionship this was a difficult adjustment for him.

Eventually he adapted and was well known as the resident tom guarding his territory.

The neighbor we interviewed had been forced to spray him with water to discourage a cat fight on her front steps. The two cats quickly separated however her relationship with the friendly male was never the same. While adjusting to life outside as a kitten he had always been fed quality treats by this neighbor. For many years this sweet male routinely dropped by for some affection during his day. Our cat lover had been forced to spray him as she was trying to prevent an injury to both males. However once sprayed, despite numerous attempts to appease him this loving male never came near her again. Even though she purchased special treats for him they were accepted with reluctance and only on the street. She had fallen from his good graces and he never approached her again. The Sociable Independent, male or female, will hold long grudges and have been known to snub their owner for short periods of time should they too inadvertently upset them.

~~*If you shamefully misuse a cat once he will always maintain a dignified reserve toward you afterward. You will never get his full confidence again.*~~ *Mark Twain*

If safely restricted to apartment life they adapt well provided they are showered with their owner's attention. The male Sociable Independent is not as welcoming to other cats as his female counterpart. It is best he remain an only cat unless he is introduced as a kitten to a companion feline or the right female kitten is provided for his entertainment. This is a male that will become broody if he is expected to share a small apartment or condominium with a newly introduced adult feline adversary. However some Sociable Independent males may be content with another compatible Feline by Design personality. It is best to consider a female kitten displaying traits of the Sophisticated Feral or Devoted Spirit.

As an inside cat safely sheltered from outside dangers he will center attention on exploring his home and focusing all affections on his beloved owner. Care must be taken to provide a stimulating environment as this boy reacts first and ponders circumstances later. There is no hidden agenda with this male. When he loves you it is with unequalled abandonment. These boys are a pleasure that command attention.

The Sociable Independent's needs are not extensive, however care must be taken if he is to remain a contented condo kitty. This Feline by Design usually adapts well to smaller spaces and will be comfortable residing in an apartment or condominium. However it is essential that his thoughtful caregiver anticipate his basic needs. He requires her presence for his security and is dependent on sources of stimulation during her absence. When alone stimulating fun will become his total focus therefore a large assortment of toys is a necessity. This personality also loves heights and should be provided with a scratching pole containing sleeping ledges. Should his pole be positioned near a window with a view he will be delighted with many hours of entertainment while alone. These males are intelligent but differ from other Feline by Design personalities in that they are totally focused on play and socializing with their owners. This male truly adores his caregiver and considers every evening as a standing engagement for time spent together. Unlike the Dignified Gentleman who carefully analyzes his world prior to reacting, this male simply reacts to every situation he encounters.

As a breeder, when a buyer desired an affectionate and loyal kitten I always suggested the warmth and loyalty that a male cat provides to their family. Many visitors to my cattery were convinced that a female cat was their only option as they feared problems from owning a male. When a buyer was selecting a kitten I was often told of the relationship they were hoping to share with their cat. If they were convinced a female was their only option I would provide information regarding each female kitten available. If a match was not found I would always introduce my first stud male London. He offered the warmth and companionship many buyers were seeking.

London was the perfect example of a Sociable Independent male. He never sprayed and insisted on sharing my bedroom birthing nook with his favorite queen while she was in delivery. He cleaned his kittens and spent long hours keeping the mother content while she was nursing their litter. Although I was a new breeder at the time I had never witnessed or read anything like this in the many "How to Breed" cat books available.

Unfortunately London was not a good stud due to the quality of kittens he threw in his first litter. However, he was an incredible example of the Sociable Independent male. To cage him would have lead to disastrous results and shortened his life. Following his only litter he was petted out to my Aunt Rose who loved and pampered him for his entire life. While he was in the cattery his personality sold many kittens. The video and pictures taken of him caring for his first and only litter continued to sell kittens for many years. Everyone wanted a male who loved both his own kittens and their mother with such unequalled dedication. Although this is not typical behavior from a stud cat it most certainly represents the loving nature of the male Sociable Independent.

Comparing Male vs. Female Sociable Independent

When asked if a female made a better pet than a male, I always answered that everything depended on the personality of the cat. In general, it has been my experience that male kittens tend to be more active while females prefer to be closer to their mother and litter mates. After a male has left the cattery and matured he usually abandons the impulsive activity of his kitten days. Many males will then focus all their love and affection on their new owner. This isn't necessarily what may be expected from a female kitten. Depending on her personality she may be withdrawn or become equally affectionate.

Therefore it is imperative that the breeder be questioned regarding both the Queen and Sire's personality. If the breeder appears obliging, request the cattery also provide personality feedback from other litters produced by the same breeding pair. If a breeder has an understanding of the Felines by Design principles she will be better able to provide assistance when selling her kittens. She will also be comfortable providing a limited example of various kitten personalities sired from each breeding pair in her cattery. The female Sociable Independent is loving and affectionate, bonding well in many varied living situations with diverse family dynamics. This ability to adapt is not always displayed in other designer females. This subject will be examined in greater detail in other publications within the Felines by Design series.

When comparing the male and female of this designer personality it becomes a personal choice when deciding on a kitten. Both male and female are loving and loyal. The Sociable Independent has an adaptable personality and will thrive in an active household. They find contentment living in a smaller space with a single owner or with a couple. Whereas the female enjoys mothering her companion cat she is equally pleased to lavish her affections solely on her owner. Although the male is sometimes better as a single cat both male and female Sociable Independent prefer an owner that is able to spend evenings and weekends at home. The male needs stimulation during his time alone whereas the female is content providing her own amusement. The male is affectionate preferring his owner's company while the female remains content with longer periods to enjoy her solitary time. The female can be finicky in her affections whereas the male is totally loyal to his preferred caregiver.

Both male and female will display displeasure by snubbing their owners when they believe they have been wronged.

Depending on the feline's unique personality and the particular situation involved it may take some time to win back any lost favor. The female will respond to an unexpected treat whereas the male will enjoy a favorite established game of play with his caregiver. Although both sexes may not appreciate when an owner has attempted to modify their cat's behavior their security is totally based on the love they share with their caregivers.

It is a wonderful experience to own either sex within this designer personality. Whether domestic or purebred you will never regret welcoming the Sociable Independent into your home.

Peter Pan

~~He remains for whole evenings on your knee, uttering his contented purr, happy to be with you and forsaking the company of his own species.~~ Theophile Gautier

As indicated by the above title, this is the cat that will remain a kitten their entire life. This designer personality is known to display great patience not always evident in other Felines by Design. They simply refuse to age or mature and will avoid confrontation at all costs. When a 'fight or flight' situation occurs they will quickly remove themselves from the impending conflict.

The female equivalent of the Peter Pan personality is known as the Precious Treasure. While the males may enjoy a little play fighting with their companion cat the females gravitate towards chasing interludes. Some are unaware of the ability to even spit as they may have avoided conflict their entire lives and will prove to be a lover and not a fighter under all circumstances.

The Peter Pan kitten is often the most mischievous of the litter. He is usually the first to awaken and is always ready for play. This is the baby his mother must closely monitor while he actively explores the nursery. In his quest for continuous kitten entertainment he often requires rescuing on a regular basis. From eating to napping to playing this feline is action driven. He possesses quick instincts and must investigate every inch of his world. This male remains a loving baby confident his needs will be met by his caring family.

~~There is no more intrepid explorer than a kitten.~~
Jules Champfleury

When personally marking their territory all cats habitually rub their sebaceous or facial scent glands against objects within their home often including their owner's legs. This behavior is referred to as bunting. With the Peter Pan personality it becomes a dedicated art, as he will not be satisfied until he has personally marked numerous objects throughout his entire home. Such marking of territory is not to be confused with the offensive spray from a stud male sometimes evident in catteries. The Peter Pan is only concerned in providing his personalized scent in those areas which he considers to be his warm and familiar territory. This scent which has been left as his friendly calling card is only obvious to other felines in the home.

~~When your cat rubs the side of his face along your leg, he's affectionately marking you with his scent, identifying you as his private property, saying, in effect, "You belong to me."~~
Susan McDonough, D.M.V.

If this male is well loved and secure in his home he will rarely exhibit behavioral problems. He is easy to please and maintains simple expectations. However he has a stubborn streak which surfaces when he is placed in any area that does not please him. Unless it was originally his personal decision he may strongly object with what his owner feels is best for him. Much like the child forced to show affection to a distant relative this male will only show resistance when he is pressured to perform outside his area of comfort. When a child is not forced to show affection but permitted a grace period of bonding they may later be discovered in the very lap of the person they refused to acknowledge. Likewise, should this cat be forced to sit with someone he is not ready to accept the same pattern will emerge. After he has decided to make his presence known only then will he place himself in the lap he originally rejected. However having settled and after enjoying an extended stay he may later require a gentle nudge to permit the visitor to leave.

When born a purebred this cat is not emotionally suited to the restricted life of a stud male. This is difficult for breeders to accept should the kitten be exceptional and set a high standard for his breed. Despite his pedigree he truly is a baby at heart and caging this male would eventually shorten his life and destroy him. Even if his own sire was an excellent stud do not attempt to change him. This kitten was intended to be a beloved altered pet and was born to live his life forever as a kitten at heart.

After several years of breeding, my best queen finally produced a top show quality male from my best sire. My sire was aging and deserved to be petted out. I finally had the right son to replace him once the kitten became proven. Within six months I realized this darling top show male was a Peter Pan. He was never bred but sold to someone who would appreciate his Peter Pan qualities and exquisite show standard. His new owner was without a feline but had once been a breeder and still loved showing. They travelled together across the country and he flourished as a top show alter in many cat shows. Over the years other breeders would contact me after seeing his continued success in numerous cat shows across the U.S. and Canada. I always advised them of my lengthy waiting list, however they insisted on being included and expressed their desire to purchase a kitten from his top show bloodline.

The Peter Pan male also sets the standard as the ultimate lap cat. This feline's unique personality appeals to everyone. More than any other Feline by Design even teenagers will acknowledge his presence with a greeting. Seniors, men, women and children are all taken with his unique child-like perspective of the world; he simply loves life. I have only encountered a few men that did not care for the sweet innocence of this designer personality. It is interesting to note that these men did not have children and never expressed an interest in doing so. This feline loves women and is very loyal and loving to the person who provides his daily care. It will be her lap he seeks for security and her presence that gives him the greatest comfort. A Peter Pan male will be devoted and faithful for the duration of his life to his beloved primary caregiver.

This is not a demanding cat seeking attention and will only become vocal when his mistress' lap is missing or he has become bored or lonely. This designer personality is not prone to overeating or weight gain. He keeps active and with sufficient stimulation during his owner's absence will remain content.

I speak from experience with this adorable male, as I am mother to both my own son Mark and to his feline brother Tally Ho. Much to Tally's chagrin, over the years Mark grew into a man while Tally forever remained a kitten. A feline with the very soul of Peter Pan, this is a carefree cat with a positive attitude and loving nature. He is easy to train and will obediently accept those off limit areas within his home which his owner may decide are unsafe for him.

In all honesty I didn't want Tally. At that point in time I simply didn't need or desire to own another cat. However there were complications with his growth as a kitten and as a responsible breeder I couldn't risk selling him. Long story short Tally was a challenge and different. Presently he is ten years old and as the years have passed I've never regretted my decision in keeping him. Tally was one of several beloved Peter Pan designer personalities who were born in my cattery.

As a kitten Tally was energetic, very active and although he was much smaller than his three brothers he possessed lightning quick instincts. This kitten was easy to please unless he became obstinate. I have often wondered if his nursing difficulties may have resulted from losing a preferred nipple to a rival kitten. Much to his mother's grief he stubbornly refused to nurse on any other nipple made available to him. This most likely was the reason for the complications with his growth. This child-like feline will still stubbornly refuse to make any changes which are not a part of his accepted and preferred routine. Changes are only possible when he believes my direction was originally his decision. Through much study and research I have since learned that this is a typical trait of the Peter Pan designer feline.

The Peter Pan personality will display traits not normally experienced with other cats. They are not always confident with their balance and therefore may not expose themselves to new height challenges. This personality is less likely to climb curtains and may never reach the top resting level of his scratching pole. However he does have a few accepted feline nuances. The novelty of sitting on the kitchen table may prove to be one of his many passing fancies. This feline craves interaction as he only learns through seeking play and stimulation within his home.

~~Cats like doors left open, in case they change their minds.~~ Rosemary Nisbet

Having owned several Peter Pans it is interesting to note that each displayed a great fascination whenever tradesmen were present in our home. Should tools be employed they would position themselves to actively watch without interfering in the actual work involved. Tally once sat for several hours on our bathroom sink watching a new tub enclosure being installed.

The tradesmen were surprised as he never moved from his position and unlike Mark did not disrupt them during their work. I was informed several times that they'd never seen a cat quite like him. I believe Tally thought it was another toy purchased just for him which was under construction, and the men had been provided simply for his amusement.

During our interviews other Peter Pan owners agreed their males also held a fascination for tools and tradesmen working within their home. One owner declared her male loved to sit on the bathroom sink every morning to watch her apply makeup before leaving for work. He displayed a particular interest in mascara and when his mistress applied it to her lashes he would close his eyes mimicking her actions. This same male insisted he have his own toothbrush and would chew on the bristles while his mistress was brushing her own teeth.

A compatible feline companion is a necessity for this designer personality. The Peter Pan loves his owner but will be unsettled without a second cat which is necessary not only for companionship but to complete his sense of self. Additionally, due to his child-like personality a companion cat will provide reassurance and comfort. It is best to seek a non-aggressive designer personality as they enjoy chasing games without any fear of confrontation. This personality is compatible with most females and some males if introduced as kittens. Should you own a feline of this nature and desire a compatible kitten, please refer to the Felines by Design compatibility chart at the beginning of this section.

Precious Treasure

~~A cat can purr her way out of anything.~~ Donna McCrohan

It was my experience that almost every visitor to our cattery was seeking one of these adorable Felines by Design. During their entire lives the Precious Treasures will remain gentle souls with sweet natured personalities. Their only desire is in dedicating themselves to providing love and companionship to their beloved owners. They are a true compliment to the male Peter Pan sharing many common traits including an especially sweet and trusting nature. The Precious Treasure loves adventure but is fearful of any confrontations. In a multi-cat household she will love every member of her feline family equally, especially those cats that will permit her a non-agressive position within the feline hierarchy of her home.

As kittens they are alert and active in pursuit of adventure as soon as they are mobile. These are gentle affectionate kittens seeking to explore the vast unknown realms of their nursery much as the Peter Pan male. They do well in peaceful multi-cat homes and will tightly bond with another mothering and gentle soul similar to themselves.

These kittens literally melt your heart and often created episodes of *kitten fever* with many buyers in my cattery. Possessing a delightful and charasmatic personality the Precious Treasure kittens were quickly sold during their first viewing. They are totally responsive to buyers and prefer being held until they have captivated their new owner's affections.

They were fascinated with the world outside the nursery. Whenever a Precious Treasure was born in my home I would carry the kitten inside my blouse while caring for the cattery. By four weeks of age I found every Precious Treasure would discover her own personalized name prior to winning the heart of her owner. By introducing the named kitten to the prospective new owner this allowed the buyer to more quickly perceive the kitten's true personality. These kittens are so incredibly sweet it was both a professional and personal challenge to part with them. Therefore as a breeder I was grateful to not be tempted into keeping one and appreciated that they sold quickly.

This is an exceptionally patient and loving Feline by Design personality. However, unlike the Peter Pan male, she may exhibit behavioral problems when forced to live in an overly stressful environment. The loud music of teenagers or excessive energy of children may unnerve her gentle soul. If she becomes uncomfortable within her home, one manner in which she may show her displeasure is by the inappropriate use of her litter box. Although the situation may only be temporary, should undue stress be the problem it will not dissipate with time or wishful thinking.

When she is in a stressful environment the stubbornness of the Peter Pan's nature surfaces as you try to persuade this sensitive girl in the rules of proper litter box etiquette. When the Precious Treasure displays an 'on again' 'off again' attitude with her litter box the source usually lies within the high activity level of the home. If her companion cat has a strong personality he may exhibit his authority by preventing her from using their common litter box. Sometimes a male companion cat will take advantage of the Precious Treasure's gentle nature. Having two boxes in separate rooms has solved this problem.

When placing one of these sensitive babies I was overly cautious with the family desiring to purchase her. It has been my experience that when this female is placed with compatible owners in a peaceful environment she is easy to please and rarely exhibits any behavioral problems.

As with the Peter Pan male this gentle female avoids confrontation at all costs. This feline may never spit to exhibit fear but will loudly purr should an adversary confront her. Often wiser than the male she prefers to confuse another feline by displaying a non-aggressive body position. Hence when challenged she holds her ground instead of displaying the more common fight or flight response. Her inability to accept a position of authority within a multi-cat household usually wins her favor and she is well loved by all. This feline does not want to be head cat under any circumstances unless she is the only cat in her home.

This queen adjusts well residing with a couple or a single person. If her owners are busy pursuing careers she will be more content and will be better suited to sharing life with a compatible and equally gentle companion cat. However, should her owners have a home based business or are working a standard day shift outside the home she will remain content as a single cat during their daily absence. The Precious Treasure will be waiting for the evenings and weekends when she will be in a position to shower them with attention. This affectionate girl is usually a devoted lap cat desiring her beloved owner's company while they are home and sleeping next to them at night. I always recommend this lovely girl for a single woman as they make an affectionate companion and always welcome the addition of a spouse should their owner decide to marry.

I have also sold this feline with great success as a companion to an older cat as she does not display territorial issues. This non-aggressive girl will also seek the company of another cat with a similar personality when she has been placed in a multi-cat environment. When she is comfortable in her home she is able to meet the needs of her owner and her companion cat. Patience is the key with this non-aggressive and affectionate female. She is a delight to own and seldom fails to locate her own human soul mate despite the space within her small world.

~~The smallest feline is a masterpiece.~~ Leonardo da Vinci

Sophisticated Feral: A Jewel in the Rough

~~Every feline is a unique and loving soul patiently waiting for the first warm touch from their chosen human soul mate.~~ Donna J. Rabinovitch

Due to the aloof and distant nature of this feline personality as a kitten both breeder and buyer often misunderstand them. Loving patience is the key as this feline is slow to trust but gradually like a blossoming flower will mature responding to her owner's affections.

They make a Perfect Condo Kitty due to their very private nature and preference for quiet peaceful spaces with a limited number of visitors. This feline simply disappears when company arrives and would never permit a Landlord to see her. Unlike other Feline by Design personalities there are few differences that surface when comparing the female Sophisticated Feral with her male counterpart.

I have owned these special kittens as domestic pets and they have also appeared in my purebred litters. As they prefer not being held these kittens are sometimes difficult to sell. However as these babies mature into adults they appear to always please their owners. They are a 'jewel in the rough' requiring a compassionate owner that is willing to permit these felines the luxury of time before bonding. This feline prefers a smaller space as she will constantly be on guard until she is comfortable in her surroundings. Unlike other felines her extreme caution must be accepted before she is willing to love her owner for a lifetime commitment. When her caregiver grants her this liberty her full loving personality will eventually emerge.

It remains a sad fact that domestic kittens are separated at a young age from their mother and litter mates. Many new owners are surprised to discover that their chosen kitten from an animal shelter or pet store displays little interest in bonding with them. When a buyer is presented with many cute babies how do you choose a warm and affectionate kitten that will become a welcomed presence within your home? Domestic litters are often the result of a feral tom and domestic queen's romantic encounter during a 'backyard breeding'. Hence, one may discover that they have adopted or purchased a Sophisticated Feral kitten.

Feral kittens are best suited for the experienced cat lover who is willing to accept these babies just as they are. Like a long anticipated wait for a fine bottle of wine, these lovely cats are exceptional when they gradually become comfortable in their home. As the Sophisticated Feral matures they remain deeply attached to their owner in a manner unlike any other Feline by Design. With time and respect the results of the bonding, although a more prolonged and individual process, are truly outstanding. Once this feline is comfortable she will permanently attach herself to her caregiver considering their relationship a lifetime commitment. The extent of their initial distant nature mirrors the extreme intimacy they will eventually share with their owner.

Just as they may have shown an initial indifference to their caregiver during the bonding process, they will remain stubborn and continue to display a strong sense of self. This feline will utilize her inherited wild instincts even after becoming comfortable within her home. My own Sophisticated Feral is a beautiful nine-year-old domestic torbie named Tia. She will strongly object when I use perfume or have a glass of wine before handling her. She trusts her nose first and only since maturing will she now accept that I am still her owner even when my scent is altered. These felines can quickly revert to their feral nature and take particular delight in chasing furry toy mice. Having thrown the mouse they become frustrated as they are convinced their prey should continue the chase and not lay still. These cats love heights and will be totally enthusiastic when their owner has provided them with a tall scratching pole with ledges.

Seldom are other kittens so extremely loyal when respecting senior cats in their home. Preferring the company of other cats they will be readily accepted into a multi-cat environment. Although the presence of other cats in a house will delay the progress of bonding with their owner, this feline is a wonderful addition as a companion cat. Should you be seeking a companion feline it is better to choose a female Sophisticated Feral regardless of the sex or personality of your present cat.

Although selective when seeking their human soul mate, once chosen their character is completely altered. Gone is the indifference and in turn the long awaited affection is showered on their owner. As this feline bonds with her caregiver slowly but surely she abandons her fear and will gradually display aspects of her personality never before revealed. In loving tones this quiet feline will begin to vocalize her true devotion which will often surprise her owner.

Well worth the time, this loving feline is a rare treat. The Sophisticated Feral should be considered as a present in disguise, a gift the owner receives by accepting her chosen baby just as she is. Given time and shown the respect she deserves this loving sweetheart will develop into a lifetime relationship as her owner's Feline Soul Mate.

This is a feline of simple pleasures. She loves her home and will appreciate any time spent in solitude while her owner works. Upon their return she may either shower them with affection or will choose to continue sleeping until she feels the need for interaction. Conversely, during a weekend at home her owner may find the most unexpected displays of vocal affection by simply entering a room where her cat has been sleeping. This female is truly an unpredictable treat providing her owner with a lifetime of warmth and entertainment.

On some level the Sophisticated Feral has a sense for adventure. However it seldom surfaces as she is usually a predictable feline that maintains a rigid schedule of sleeping, eating and loving interaction with her caregiver. As she is a timid soul at heart her outdoor life is more comfortably suited to an enclosed apartment balcony. More often than not she will vocalize her desire to only share this special outdoor retreat with company. Although the enclosed balcony is a part of her treasured territory she is only comfortable when it is shared with her owner.

Every breeder will have kittens she cannot relate to and does not find endearing. There is even a sense of guilt when you sell such a baby because you wonder if anyone can bond with this kitten. A purebred feline is an expensive investment. How then can you accept payment for a kitten that may never truly desire or become a loving family member? This was a dilemma I faced as a new cat breeder. What should I do with a feral kitten that will not allow you to touch them?

As a breeder I experienced only a few feral kittens in my breeding program. I was working with Himalayan and Persian cats from unrelated bloodlines. Despite the Sire and Dam used, occasionally a feral kitten would be born in a litter of loving and responsive babies. It has been my experience that with the right person these babies eventually learned to love and trust their owners. Once they have been removed from the cattery and are the only feline in their new home they make great progress.

Such was my first experience with a feral Blue Point Himalayan male purchased by a French Canadian couple. He was from a single kitten litter and would only interact with his mother. This male ignored kittens from my other litters and kept his distance from me. However he was the last Himalayan available and the only baby this couple was interested in buying. For the wife it was simply love at first sight. I had some reservations as to whether the love affair would last once he was in their home.

After I saw him the following year this lovely male provided a valuable lesson in feline bonding. He was given uncondi-tional love from his owners and while I had never been able to hold him he responded to them with great affection. It was a wonderful experience to see this once emotionally detached male sharing such love and devotion with his mistress. They had named him Saphir and with their nuturing love and affection he had grown into a Saphire jewel of the highest quality.

Unconditional love and patience in a quiet environment will greatly assist bonding with the Sophisticated Feral. Male or female, purebred or domestic, the memory of these lovely cats lingers with their owners for the duration of their lives. It is yet to be determined whether the key lies in the longer bonding time required to gain their affection or the complexity of their gentle personalities. For those willing to explore and understand the Sophisticated Feral, their reward will be in obtaining a feline's love unlike any other Feline by Design.

~~When she walked... she stretched out long and thin like a little tiger, and held her head high to look over the grass as if she were treading the jungle.~~ Sarah Orne Jewett

Bewitching Goddess

~~Cats, as a class, have never completely got over the snootiness caused by the fact that in Ancient Egypt they were worshipped as gods.~~ P.G. Wodehouse

This is a Feline by Design possessing such a 'take command' presence that she usually holds the position of head cat in her home. Whether living as a single feline or in a multi-cat residence she is self-assured and secure in any environment presented as her home. I am well acquainted with this Feline by Design having known this personality as a kitten, breeding queen and as a domestic feline. She rarely exhibits behavioral problems with the exception of her strong nature while preserving her presence as head family cat.

As a kitten she quickly assesses her new home environment and never fails to have her every want and need met. She is not a lap cat by nature but when her mood dictates will sit for hours with her mistress displaying unaccustomed affection. Over time this intelligent queen will instinctively entice each family member into meeting her various needs. One will be favored for warmth and cuddling at night while another may be selected for exercise during playful interludes. The successful results are that this girl will equally endear herself to every member of her family. However her beloved mistress is of prime importance for her emotional security as she is the one who provides her daily basic care.

This lovely girl does well in various family environments being equally content in a busy household with respectful children or when residing with one owner in a smaller space. As an only cat she thrives as the center of attention. When there are no other pets in her home she will routinely seek various family members for stimulation depending on her mood. This queen is an amusing, perplexing and interesting feline to own. Although vocally demanding when her needs are not met she is not a noisy cat by nature. Of particular interest is this feline's elevated sense of self-esteem. In my experience both men and women who are attracted to this female are captivated by her free spirit with the ability to command her own world and make things happen.

She travels well responding favorably to changes in residence and the addition of a spouse should her owner wish to marry. She especially enjoys the stimulation of company and will center herself to entertain when visitors arrive. My own Bewitching Goddess loved travelling to cat shows across the U.S. and Canada. She would routinely bewitch the judges and charm anyone passing by her show cage.

Throughout the other Feline by Design profiles I have employed various adjectives such as engaging, affectionate, mothering and sensitive. However such terms do not adequately capture the essence of this exceptionally captivating queen. She is an entertaining and beloved energy of self-assurance. She loves everyone but only on her terms, which like the weather often varies. The kittens I have sold display-ing this engaging personality were never returned. Such babies quickly charm their owners and reign supreme as the Bewitching Goddess within their homes.

These felines are not difficult nor have complex personalities. One rarely misunderstands their intentions and soon learns to appreciate their unique concept of the world. They demand attention or peace and quiet without creating any fuss or bother for their owners. This is the kitten that is self-sufficient and will do quite well as her owner pursues a career working long hours. She relies on her quick instincts and does not need constant supervision or extended company to keep her content. Upon her owner's arrival home this queen readily changes gears exchanging love and interaction with the presentation of fresh food and water.

Her needs are simple providing her needs are quickly met. Despite this feline's strong sense of self she will draw upon her playful nature to partake in a regular session of catnip play. The Bewitching Goddess enjoys enhancing the bond shared with her mistress and will repeatedly retrieve a tossed furry toy mouse for hours of fun and exercise. If her mistress must work long hours for business this queen will insist any time at home is sacred and should be reserved solely for their mutual enjoyment. She will remain quite adamant that in exchange for long hours alone at home her mistress must provide love and attention when they share time together.

It has been my experience that the Bewitching Goddess, whether purebred or domestic are the most physically beautiful cats I have ever encountered. With such great beauty they are always noticed and constantly admired. Perhaps their vanity and strong sense of self is partially due to a lifetime of verbal compliments received. They walk in beauty and carry themselves with diplomatic dignity. These felines are only demanding when their mistress may have forgotten to change their water or neglected to supply an expected treat upon their arrival home. They are accustomed to the occasional indulgence by their owner and repay any kindness with much love and attention. This feline possesses great faith in her family and an even greater faith in a life filled with total love and pampering. They lead a blessed life and appear to understand their high level of importance in their families. "You are mine, therefore I am loved," appears to be their approach to living and in turn is truly their lifetime mantra.

~~There's no need for a piece of sculpture in a home that has a cat.~~ Wesley Bates

Feline Zeus

~~Cats, particularly male cats, like very strong names which link them to majestic feats.~~ Auriel Douglas

The Feline Zeus male shares many of the characteristics of his female counterpart the Bewitching Goddess. He is both a leader and a lover within his home depending solely on his mood of the moment. Whereas the Bewitching Goddess walks in beauty this is a physically strong and powerful male. He is beloved to some and intimidating to others.

Firstly, it must be understood that this cat is best suited to living in a home without children. Once matched with a compatible owner the best qualities of this male will be realized. He bonds quite well with a single woman or bachelor living alone in a smaller space. If he is owned by a couple not wishing to have children he can be quite content and will love them both equally. When considering this dynamic and robust Feline by Design personality the owner should be comfortable with their present living arrangements. It must be noted that this male may not accept the addition of a spouse should his owner decide to marry. Hence an equally strong man or woman desiring a career over the commitment of marriage and family often selects him.

As a kitten these males march to the beat of their own drum. They seldom bond to or will display affection with their breeders. These are only one of several Feline by Design personalities that commonly display such aloof characteristics.

Such babies prefer to only explore the nursery and play with their litter mates avoiding human contact as much as possible. However when the right owner has purchased them the bonding occurs quickly and is a satisfying experience for both feline and new owner. The secret lies within the breeder's ability to both recognize the Feline Zeus as a kitten and assess the qualities that will provide a satisfying bonding experience with the right owner.

This baby does not resemble the Sophisticated Feral who characteristically displays a prolonged and fearful distrust of her environment. The Feline Zeus is both fearless and strong willed. He displays little interest in socializing as he simply prefers the company of his mother and litter mates while in the nursery. Once placed in a loving home and honored as the glorious cat he perceives himself to be the bonding with his caregiver is a delight to behold.

Unless a breeder is experienced she may not realize the special needs this male requires with his owner. Such a male simply does better as an only cat relating with a single owner. He will be equally content if chosen by a couple preferring a peaceful and quiet home. Although an intense cat by nature, when he has bonded with his owner the relationship will truly be a meeting of the minds. Those owners loved by these males are high in praise confident that no other feline has ever completed their home with such dignity.

This male displays high intelligence and is not difficult to please as he usually prefers to please himself. Much like the Bewitching Goddess he needs time alone which is usually a trait shared with his working owner. He is best suited for condo or apartment life residing alone while his owner pursues a career necessitating extended hours away from home. While at home his caregiver's time should include meeting this male's emotional needs so that he will remain content and satisfied.

One has heard the expression "a man's man." Such a term

can equally be applied to this intensely thought provoking male. He is the Feline by Design displaying the very strongest traits of the male cat. For example, every breeder prefers a stud male with the same self-assurance and ability to remain content while residing within a smaller space. Due to his aloof nature as an unaltered tom he is one of the better choices for a cattery. This is the stud male that will remain content provided he is well cared for in a good cattery. He will be excellent for breeding and in a reasonably sized nook will remain satisfied with the life of an active stud male.

Much as his name implies, the Feline Zeus shares characteristics with the well-known Zeus in Greek Mythology. Zeus too had a weakness - he was passionately fond of female charms. Many stories about Zeus recount his insatiable lust and notorious wandering eye, an eye that fell upon goddess and mortal woman alike. Hence the Feline Zeus will weave the same magic spell upon his breeding queens or that one special mortal woman that claims him for her own.

~~Way down deep, we're all motivated by the same urges. Cats have the courage to live by them~~ Jim Davis

The best is realized from this male when introduced as a kitten to his new home. When receiving affection as a young kitten he adapts well and will be equally content with a single owner or couple. Once successfully matched, even as an adult this male will be extremely affectionate with his chosen owner. With this particular Feline by Design he personally selects his owner and with time their bond will be intensely complete.

Much as with the Bewitching Goddess, the Feline Zeus is equally charming with his own mistress. His needs are simple and he is never a difficult feline to please. This male tends to sleep long hours and therefore may have a tendency for weight gain. If he has a stimulating environment with a scratching pole containing sleeping ledges he will enjoy climbing as exercise. When his diet is closely monitored with a good quality food, weight gain should not be a problem.

I have owned one stud male and sold many kittens with this designer personality. Despite many attempts to share love with my breeding male he chose not to be affectionate with me. Eventually I was no longer able to use him in my breeding program and he was sold to another cattery. To my total amazement he loved and bonded quickly with his new breeder. When visiting him it was truly a wonderful experience to watch how he responded with limitless affection to her which had always been denied to me. As mentioned these males truly select the owner they desire to love. Feline Zeus kittens grow into engaging males. Much as their bewitching female counterparts they are only vocally demanding when their needs are not met.

One Feline Zeus owner noted that her male was spoiled as a kitten and enjoyed watching the sunrise from his apartment's glass enclosed balcony. During the early morning hours he would demand the balcony door be opened at 4:00 a.m. by sitting on his mistress' chest until she rose to satisfy his needs. She soon learned to anticipate his desires by leaving the balcony door open prior to retiring for the night and was able to enjoy an undisturbed sleep.

Owners of Feline Zeus kittens have always reported their delight in the quirky nature of their males. Several women informed me that living with a Feline Zeus was as engaging as living with a loving husband. They learn to think as their owners and are quite aware when their mistress may be unsettled and require special attention. Women describe the intensity of their intimate relationship with the Feline Zeus as follows: "I'll only own a male cat after loving him", "He's better than a husband" or "He never complains when I work over time." Although this male is not to everyone's taste he is beloved by those who have taken him as their feline of choice. To be selected as the owner of a Feline Zeus is to find true love and contentment with a male cat.

~~The cat has been described as the most perfect animal, the acme of muscular perfection and the supreme example in the animal kingdom of the coordination of mind and muscle~~ Roseanne Ambrose

Lovable Teddy Bear

~~Who can believe that there is no soul behind those luminous eyes!~~ Theophile Gautier

Whenever I research material for additional books it becomes pure delight when I encounter this Feline by Design. The warm memories I have shared with this endearing personality tend to overwhelm me during the first few minutes of any interview with their owner. Many years ago, as a new breeder I had the pleasure of owning one of these lovely boys as my primary stud cat. It was due to his personable nature and my passion for his Feline by Design personality that his kittens were usually sold prior to conception.

My experience with the domestic variation of Lovable Teddy Bears further evolved through one long-term friendship. Whenever Pat had to travel for business I would always move into her home to care for her diabetic tabby named Barney. I soon grew to appreciate the qualities of this engaging male and to understand his unique perspective of the world. These are fun loving boys who will often engage in mischievous activity to obtain their mistress' attention. They are also one of the more sensitive males and should they feel they have been mistreated with excessive discipline will either sulk or display other temporary aspects of feline depression.

As their name implies this Feline by Design is the truest of lovers. With a great passion they actively seek and will display affection to their immediate family members. However, they are more timid with visitors and prefer to observe company from a safe distance away. Lovable Teddy Bears tend to be larger cats having a primary passion for satisfying their stomachs. Hence due to their appetites they usually resemble what is referred to as carrying the Lovable Teddy Bear physique. To know them is to love them for they are easy care cats requesting little more than love and affection from their families.

While in the nursery this kitten enjoys interacting and being handled by his breeder. Although once returned to his mother he may appear more at ease in the company of his litter mates. After his litter has been shown several times this designer baby will warmly respond to visitors viewing the cattery. However some Lovable Teddy Bear kittens may only display true contentment when they are placed next to the reassuring presence of their mothers. Unless the breeder showcases the endearing qualities of this baby he may be overlooked due to a more openly forward kitten.

Between four and six weeks of age this baby prefers cuddling with his mother over the gentle handling and interacting with buyers. He should never be confused with his more fearful and distant litter mate, the Sophisticated Feral. The Lovable Teddy Bear has an affectionate nature filled with love for the person who will open their heart to him.

For those seeking such a kitten it is best to question the breeder regarding the other notable qualities of this lovely boy. He will cautiously explore the nursery but not with the same passion as his brother, the Peter Pan male. He is perceptive and intelligent but not as forward as his litter mate the Sociable Independent. This is the sensitive darling that appears slightly hesitant but will eventually respond with warm purrs as he is gently held in a buyer's hands. From my experience this male kitten is never a disappointment always completing his family with warmth, love and a life long dedication.

These males do well in a family environment and are comfortable residing in smaller spaces. Single women and men are drawn to this Feline by Design due to their quiet nature and ease of care. These males seldom display behavioral problems but require more hands on care and company than the more self-assured Feline Zeus. Whereas the Feline Zeus is content with his own company for longer periods of time during the day, the Lovable Teddy Bear prefers an environment where his owners work a standard shift and spend more time at home.

The Lovable Teddy Bear is perfectly suited for apartment and condo life. He adores women but equally appeals to a single man who may be tired of returning home to an empty apartment. For the bachelor this cat becomes a buddy who enjoys shared evenings watching the latest sports event on television. For a woman residing alone, the Teddy Bear will snuggle close whenever he senses she has experienced a difficult day. In an attempt to provide additional comfort, a typical trait of the Teddy Bear is to climb into his mistress' lap and rest his head under her chin. This adorable male simply won't leave his owner's side until he has comforted her. This is a male that will always welcome the addition of a spouse when his owner decides to marry. Couples also praise the attributes of this adorable fellow because in their home his presence compliments their intimate circle.

Many of my Lovable Teddy Bear kittens were bred or descended from my beloved stud male Chadwick. I never knew Chadwick as a kitten but having raised several of his litters I came to realize what an incredible kitten he must have been. As a breeder, these babies were simply delightful and it was a pleasure to showcase his kittens. As an active stud male Chadwick had unique and specific requirements during breeding season. After feeding him it was a necessity to remove his food dish before he would take an active interest in breeding. Even when placed with his favorite queen, a Bewitching Goddess named Candace, he would literally climb over her back to reach the remnants of his dinner. As far as he was concerned, sex of course had it's place but only after satisfying his stomach.

~~Even overweight, cats instinctively know the cardinal rule: when fat, arrange yourself in slim poses.~~ John Weitz

These males are passive yet playful. To my good fortune Chadwick was one of those rare stud males that never sprayed. While the cattery was under renovations he had the opportunity to stay in a dear friend's apartment. He thoroughly enjoyed life as a condo kitty and experiencing time as a pet cat. My friend loved his company so much she requested if Chadwick's stay could be extended until he was required in the cattery for the next breeding season. These adorable males are good natured and seldom create problems in their homes even as stud cats. Due to his placid and affectionate nature Chadwick was given freedom of movement within the cattery during the day but returned to his nook at night. However that privilege was only extended to him when my queens were not calling during our non-breeding months.

As mentioned earlier, my friend Pat also owned this delightful Feline by Design personality. Since Barney was diabetic I cared for him when she travelled on business. Eventually he permitted me to interact with him and I grew to love and appreciate the unique qualities of this model Lovable Teddy Bear. Although it may take time, these males eventually gravitate towards anyone pursuing a genuine interest in them. Only following careful observation and studying a returning visitor to their home will they make an effort to introduce themselves. They will make their approach to investigate and befriend the guest once they have decided a visitor is kind and non-threatening. I further discovered that it hastens the process to spoil them with an unexpected cat gift once in a while.

To truly understand this feline it should be realized that he demonstrates persistence when seeking a personalized area within his home. Being a deeply sensitive male, a loud voice or sharp words of criticism will have a profound emotional effect on him. Expect this male to disappear for long periods of time when he believes his owner is displeased with him.

Should sleeping on your dining room table be of interest to him but unacceptable to you, a sharp loud voice to discourage his behavior will not be effective. His owner soon learns that repetitive verbal discipline only triggers his stubborn streak and not the desired behavior. A more productive approach with this designer personality is achieved by applying the gentle touch. It is more effective to both quietly and physically remove him from an unsafe area by redirecting his interest to a safer place.

When an owner uses loud verbal discipline this male will quickly retreat in fear. However once his attention has been drawn to the restricted area, he will eventually be drawn back to re-offend. To deflect his attention from an undesired area of interest his owner should make immediate changes to the cat's environment. If it was the height of the dining room table that was the initial attraction then create a tempting area of feline interest that also incorporates height. In order to satisfy his desire to climb, purchase a scratching pole with sleeping ledges which will then become his primary focus for enjoyment. He will claim the scratching pole as his personal domain and it will become his preference for observation and playful exercise. Hence when purchasing one of these darling boys I strongly recommend their owner have a scratching pole with sleeping ledges to satisfy this basic need in their developing kitten.

When considering a diet necessary to maintain good health this is a male that will be satisfied with any product purchased for him. Despite his non-finicky approach to food it is a better investment to always purchase the most nutritional products. Cat foods that provide sound nutrition tend to satisfy felines and they will be content consuming smaller portions. When a cat overeats due to a product containing inferior nutrition it may develop into an unhealthy lifetime habit.

I purchased Chadwick as an unproven male from a prominent show judge within my National Cat Association. He was ten months of age and had been restricted to a caged existence from the time he had matured. After purchasing him and driving the long distance back to our home he remained unsettled and refused to eat for several days. I was concerned and contacted his breeder only to be informed that Chadwick loved food and was not difficult to please. He had always been fed a home brew concoction of cat food his entire life. In order to save money this registered show judge cooked cat food in his kitchen and fed his entire cattery including all his kittens with an inferior diet providing little nutrition.

I realized after owning him for a short period of time that Chadwick's rate of consumption appeared to be emotionally triggered. Under my care he was fed a high quality veterinarian prescribed diet which he accepted and grew to love. However the pattern of receiving a substandard diet of cooked food during his most important period of development had already determined his eating patterns for life. Chadwick, my beloved boy only lived to be four years of age. He died in his sleep lying next to me one evening in the same bedroom where many of his kittens had been born. His loss was very sudden and totally unexpected. He may have been a valuable stud male in my breeding program but more importantly he was also my beloved boy. Our incredible veterinarian Dr. George performed an autopsy without charge the following day. As a breeder, Chadwick's short life was one of the most important messages I would pass along to clients purchasing kittens from my cattery.

Dr. George's findings determined that due to a poor quality diet as a kitten this lovely boy had been deprived of good nutrition and his heart never developed properly. He insisted I was not to blame myself nor had the cattery been exposed to a virus which had been my initial fear. If you are purchasing a kitten it is mandatory to determine the quality of diet your baby has been receiving. The same diet will have been provided to his parents and therefore his start in life will be further determined by the diet they received. Chadwick would have lived a longer life had the judge provided his cattery with a better diet purchased with a veterinarian's endorsement. Chadwick was both a stud male and my beloved companion. There are many breeders such as myself that always remember and deeply mourn the loss of their breeding felines.

With young kittens it is mandatory that breeders provide a good quality diet to encourage healthy growth. As an owner, when purchasing your kitten it is important to continue the same high quality diet as recommended by your veterinarian. Should your adult feline encounter weight gain consult your vet to determine a certified diet that will contain nutrition but be lower in fat and calories. I personally prefer to never decrease the amount of food provided but decrease calorie intake through fat content only. An adult cat fed a high quality diet containing fewer fat and calories and provided with the opportunity and space to exercise will safely lose weight. Your veterinarian is best to advise of the correct diet for your feline and should also be consulted before changing your cat's dietary requirements.

The Lovable Teddy Bear often needs to be prompted to indulge in exercise and play. Far removed from his feral kin and with the days of kittenhood long over this boy needs stimulation through the introduction of clever toys that will tease him into action. Not all Lovable Teddy Bears consider sleeping a high priority. However many will partake in restful slumber until the very moment they hear their owner's key unlocking their apartment door. Some owners interviewed claim their males were in the exact same position when they returned in the evenings as when they left for work in the morning. A companion kitten may be a consideration to keep this boy active if he tends to sleep long hours while his owner is not home.

A Lovable Teddy Bear will respond well to a companion kitten even when he has been an only cat for several years.

Due to his sensitive nature it is best to consider a loving queen that will compliment his gentle approach to life. For successful results when sharing his home with a compatible feline consult our Perfect Condo Kitty Personality Guide on page 56.

Having owned Chadwick I must confess that this endearing Feline by Design is a particular favorite of mine. Tally Ho, my Peter Pan male is Chadwick's grandson. Every once in a while Tally will mimic a loving gesture that reminds me of his grandfather. When you have been breeding for any length of time you never forget those special felines that formed your breeding program. Breeders can be haunted years later when generations are born with similar physical or personal characteristics of a beloved and lost feline.

For those seeking this treasure of a feline he can be recognized in both domestic and purebred litters. This male is a joy to own and never fails to leave his home without permanently touching the heart of every family member. Chadwick is one dear beloved soul I hope to see again when it is my time to also cross the Rainbow Bridge.

~~Cat's eyes seem a bridge to a world beyond the one we know.~~ Lynn Hollyn

Devoted Spirit

After living in a cattery for many years it was a fascinating study to observe the personality traits of my varied Felines by Design. Through the process of interviewing cat owners and from my own experiences with each designer personality I discovered that many couplings were linked and made ideal male/female combinations. For example, the Peter Pan male and Precious Treasure female shared many traits as did the Feline Zeus with his own female counterpart the Bewitching Goddess. Although not always suited as companions for each other they were ideally matched and had similar auras that projected the same energy flow. The Ying/Yang aspects of their specific sex further complimented each personality. It became an important consideration when studying the Ying/Yang theory of striking a balance between the passive feminine and the active masculine side of a cat's nature.

Following months of research, as I enhanced other personality profiles, I suddenly realized how the Lovable Teddy Bear was uniquely connected to the sensitive Devoted Spirit. Although I had been writing and combining the various designer felines by sex for several months I had never directly connected these two loving personalities.

~~I put down my book, The Meaning of Zen, and see the cat smiling into her fur as she delicately combs it with her rough pink tongue. Cat, I would lend you this book to study but it appears you have already read it. She looks up and gives me full gaze... Don't be ridiculous, she purrs, I wrote it.~~
from "Miao" by Dilys Laing

I was blessed with my own two Devoted Spirits, Liberty and Dana who equally touched my heart in much the same way as my darling Chadwick. What first drew me to these most feminine of the Felines by Design was their quiet dignity. These are queens possessing great character despite their sensitive and reserved nature.

As an owner of these two classic beauties, they always presented themselves as spiritual mysteries to me. I wanted to draw them closer but sensed their need for distance. Therefore I reluctantly gave them the space they needed. Although I knew each queen well and sensed their obvious love for me, they appeared to present an aura of:

~~You are a Human and I am a Cat, how can you understand my ways.~~ Donna J. Rabinovitch

I accepted those terms but I always felt the need to cuddle and draw them physically closer, especially as they lay next to me in the evenings. I believe they sensed my total love and devotion and therefore from time to time I was permitted a limited period of intimate contact with them. One benefit of residing in a home with many felines is that your lap is never empty when sitting down. However when one of my Devoted Spirits sought an affectionate cuddle I would suspend any household or cattery duties to sit and hold them close. I've never regretted those moments.

~~Housework will be around when I am dead and gone but the life of a feline is fleeting.~~ Isabell Ann Kinnear

Therefore listening to my grandmother's words of wisdom, I chose to hold them for as long as they would sit with me. When a cat is truly loved by their owner, her affection will eventually develop into an emotional commitment. When you are a breeder and spend long hours soothing a queen while they kitten, that bond mutually develops into an intense commitment. The beautiful Devoted Spirit whether nuturing her kittens or nuturing her owner is a queen that defies description. Describing a relationship with this personality further prejudices me as I was in total awe and so in love with my own. This female makes her owner feel selected and special as she refuses to share her affections with others. You simply know that she holds you in high esteem and is grateful for every kind act you bestow upon her. Even the daily rituals of refreshing her water, replacing her food and keeping her litter box clean are deeply appreciated. She is aware of everything within her environment and as her owner you never feel taken for granted. Whereas the Bewitching Goddess demands her needs be met simply because you are her caregiver, the Devoted Spirit is extremely grateful for every kindness bestowed upon her.

This gentle and sensitive kitten will present herself in the nursery much as the Lovable Teddy Bear male. She too will explore but is always the first drawn back to rest next to her

FELINES BY DESIGN

mother leaving her litter mates actively at play. She prefers sharing private moments with her mother, the center of her world and needs reflective time to study her environment. She responds warmly with her breeder but never appears truly at ease away from the comforting presence of her mother.

I have witnessed those perceptive buyers that seem to understand there is depth to this gentle sweetheart. During the first viewing they recognize a kindred spirit dwells within this lovely kitten and will not consider any other baby. Many buyers quickly make their choice and will leave a deposit to ensure they will share their home with this darling girl. Even as kittens, many buyers perceive their unique qualities and are drawn to this feline's depth of soul and character. Although the Devoted Spirit will often appear skittish it may be that she is still processing the activity within the sheltered world of her nursery.

Even as babes these girls are intellectual sponges. They enjoy playing with their litter mates but remain alert and learn from observing all that occurs within the limited world of their nursery. As this designer personality tends to project their fear of the unknown, they prefer to withdraw in quiet contemplation. With maturity the Devoted Spirit eventually becomes comfortable and will begin to socialize after studying life outside their nursery nook. Once they understand the routine of the nursery they will become more socially active within their litter. Never desiring the role of lead kitten they discover their own way to quietly explore their world. I found another gentle kitten would always follow her lead, as the Devoted Spirit would discover the quiet unknown areas of the nursery often overlooked by the more zealous kittens.

These beautiful queens are sensitive and natural mothers. If your choice is this spiritual feline you will never regret the time taken to win her heart. They are proud to be cats and as their owner it will take some time before you feel their absolute trust and acceptance. Only after many years have passed will they totally relinquish their guard and trust the love you have provided for them within your home. The Devoted Spirit is deeply committed, and with mutual respect shared will openly show the affection and adoration they feel for their owner.

Due to their very private nature they make Perfect Condo Kitties as they actually prefer their homes to be smaller spaces. They feel more secure in an apartment, condominium or townhouse which provide limited change or social activity. This female will do well as a single cat or as a companion cat to many other Felines by Design due to her sweet essence as a non-agressive cat. Women are usually drawn to this sensitive soul, however bachelors have also purchased this designer kitten with equal success. Due to her nature she prefers a home without dogs and children but will readily accept a marriage partner when her owner has decided the time is right.

This queen lives her life in a divided world. She is both a secretive feline and beloved pet. When the feral nature of this lovely girl overwhelms her she will play a game I called "Wild Kitty." Liberty loved to hide in my basement for up to a week preferring to be a wild cat in total seclusion. Once I had determined this was the time for her twice yearly emotional sabbatical I respected her wishes. The house I rented had a large hidden area under the staircase where boxes and assorted unused materials were stored. This became Liberty's choice for her private sabbatical. Under the stairs she was safe and could hear the soothing activity of the cattery while she pondered her private world. Her preference during her self-imposed sabbatical was to wander the entire house under the cloak of darkness. I would also play the game and we totally ignored the other's presence if by chance we encountered each other in the darkened hallway.

To make her experience more enjoyable I would leave fresh food, water and a private litter box near her personal area of seclusion. About a week later Liberty would suddenly appear full of love and affection by bounding on my bed quite content to rejoin her family. She would always thank me for taking care of her when she needed her retreat and for days would permit me to hold and cuddle her. Had I the experience then as I do now I would have taken additional care to document the time she required to reach such high levels of personal fulfillment. I wonder now why she retreated when she did and if there was any pattern that may have occurred within the cattery that triggered her need for seclusion. Other owners have informed me that they too have encountered periods of time when their queen would also remain hidden. Depending on their living space it may simply be under a bed or couch or a more secluded area such as under our basement stairs. This was only one of the many mysteries this lovely designer personality presented to me as a novice breeder.

I am captivated by this Feline by Design because in my breeding experience she is the most nuturing and devoted of mothers. They affect me in such a profound way, touching that private area of my heart reserved solely for my husband and son. I have personally owned two such females who became breeding queens in my cattery. The first arrived as a sixteen-week-old Himalayan kitten from New York whom we named Liberty. The second I later acquired as an eight-month-old white Persian and was named Danaluk.

Poor Danaluk had suffered through an abusive start in life. She was purchased from a cattery where she was never permitted to live outside the confinement of a cage. It is important to understand that when naming a cat you are drawing Universal energy into that feline's life. As a feline responds to their name they also absorb the positive or negative energy that their owner has attached to the name. Therefore Danaluk was quickly changed to a softer variation and she was re-named Dana. I was enriched by the presence of this beautiful feline in my life and with a softer name I was hopeful she would come to trust people again.

Dana's story was highlighted in the first volume of the

Felines by Design series entitled **Proven Marketing Tips for the Successful Cat Breeder**. She was one of three felines I purchased at a low price due to their infliction with the ringworm virus and their breeder's disinterest in their time consuming and costly medical care. Dana experienced a difficult start in life and had never been loved or handled by anyone. I was drawn to her because she needed affectionate handling however she was terribly fearful of life outside her cage. She would only respond to me when I gently spoke to her while she remained separated by the safety of her cage. What haunted and drew me constantly back to her confinement was the pain I saw in her eyes. I'd seen that same expression in my own eyes reflected back from my bathroom mirror. I too had known that same fear from living with the ghosts of a difficult past. Alone in the world I was working endless hours trying to support my son and myself on a limited income. To encounter a beautiful cat that seemed to mirror my own journey in life was a haunting experience. Dana's incredible story will be expanded in future publications as her life greatly affected my own.

~~Cats are glorious creatures... who must on no accounts be underestimated... Their eyes are fathomless depths of cat world mysteries.~~ Lesley Anne Ivory

As a novice breeder Liberty was my first experience with this loving personality. She arrived with her litter sister Chantal and became an education in the complexity of this beloved personality. Dana and Liberty were two incredible mothers who eventually formed the nucleus of my cattery. I was shown how the love between a breeding feline could be as intense as that shared with a treasured pet cat. Due to the many Devoted Spirit kittens each queen produced in my breeding program, I was able to interview other owners who shared their hearts and homes with this unique designer personality.

Whether a breeding female or loving pet, after sharing your

life with this reflective female she will never cease to surprise you. Just when you believe you fully understand her feline ways you will discover there are even more complex areas of her heart to comprehend. Although she loves deeply and sincerely there is always a margin of distance she requires to safeguard her private thoughts. Just as a teenage girl keeps a locked journal of her most private feelings so does this queen guard areas of her life away from her beloved owner. Both Dana and Liberty never failed to catch me off guard with their high level of intelligence and sensitivity. This writer will explore this sensitive designer personality in future publications.

It is best to say that the memory of these secretive, loving and guarded queens have remained with me for many years since I have laid them both to rest. These secretive felines possess a profound emotional connection where their memory remains locked within their owners' hearts for a lifetime. When this queen welcomes you into her world it is with total love and acceptance. Their trust is like a blossoming flower. Year after year they reveal their depth of affection and loyalty to their special entrusted caregiver. As time passes their cherished, trusted and special owner will become the center of their universe. This feline is so complete in her perception of the world that should her owner be the only human contact she ever encountered, it would be more than sufficient to keep her content and satisfied for her lifetime.

~~When you're special to a cat, you're special indeed... she brings to you the gift of her preference of you, the sight of you, the sound of your voice, the touch of your hand.~~
Lenore Fleischer

Feline Chameleon

~~No one can own a cat, but they will bless you with their company, if they choose.~~ Frank Engram

As their Feline by Design name indicates this cat blends well and finds contentment in numerous family situations. I have seen this personality surface in both purebred and domestic litters with little difference in personality to distinguish the male from the female Chameleon.

Although both the male and female within this designer personality are sweet cats they will rarely bond with their breeders. They require time to mature and spend their days in the nursery playing with litter mates and enjoying their mother's care. Many Feline Chameleons will pass through a cattery leaving little imprint in the memory of their breeders. Although she was the first person to handle them with tender care, this kitten prefers to be with his mother and desires less contact from his breeder. I have known these kittens to assume the position of lead kitten in their litters or be equally content in the role of following a stronger willed sibling.

This intriguing Feline by Design baby initially appears as a blank canvas. As kittens some may range from possessing a timid nature to others appearing stronger willed. However despite this vast range every kitten within this designer personality will share a common characteristic. Once they have been purchased and are introduced to their new home they become a reflection and totally absorb the essence of their owner. It has been my experience that those fortunate to select this distinctive kitten are always satisfied with their choice. This kitten matures into an adult that basically reflects the personality of their owner. Such matches are made in heaven and those that select this feline are truly delighted with their choice.

Feline Chameleon kittens thrive in smaller spaces. They are content residing with couples and make wonderful company for single men or women. They adapt well when alone and enjoy peace and quiet in their apartments while their owners work a standard day shift. However time with their owner is important to them and this feline will insist on attention once their owner has returned in the evenings and on weekends. They are a relatively easy care feline and as they reflect their owner's personality, seldom display behavioral problems. Unless this designer personality is chosen by a couple as a kitten, they may be selective with their affections should their owner decide to marry. However much is determined by their beloved owner's choice whether it is the addition of a spouse or a companion feline for their enjoyment. An owner's bonding with this feline is so personal and intense that it becomes an instinctive choice for both. If their owner is truly content with a marriage partner their Feline Chameleon will also absorb the same contentment. Not all designer personalities are this easy to please.

Several of my girlfriends were drawn to this interesting personality and chose their Chameleon babies when they were four to six weeks of age. Therefore I was granted a rare opportunity to observe these kittens as they grew to maturity and gradually bonded with their owners. One particular Chameleon with a sense of independence was born in my second litter and I met a dear friend through that connection. Following the purchase Fay visited her kitten several times a week and our friendship developed over time. She was a mature woman who had never married and was seeking companionship through a loving feline connection.

I was a young, novice breeder still learning valuable lessons in cattery management and interpreting the emerging personalities of my kittens. One very important lesson for all breeders to learn is that not every kitten will desire to bond with you or will want your loving attention. The male Fay selected did not welcome my touch and seemed to only tolerate my attempts of affection with him. I worried my friend would eventually be disappointed with his inability to display affection after he was introduced to his new home. With age comes wisdom and I have learned that most of the worrying we do in life is truly wasted energy. We are literally borrowing tomorrow's troubles before their time. Such were my worries with my friend and this odd strong willed little kitten. He is what I would later identify as the truest form of a Feline Chameleon.

A few days after Roberto left the cattery he quickly bonded with his new mistress. They shared a relationship so intense I would fondly tell her it was better than many marriages I had observed. My girlfriend was a true cat lover and had lived for several years without satisfying her desire for feline companionship. Fay gave unconditional love to Roberto providing the best of everything for him and expected little in return. However once settled within his loving environment he quickly responded to her affection and kindness. Although Fay initially appeared to have a tough exterior she was truly a warm person with a heart of gold. Whether this male responded to the unconditional love or recognized a kindred spirit was beyond my knowledge at the time. I would watch them interact over the years and marvelled at the depth of their mutual understanding of each other. Roberto became her Feline Soul Mate. As a breeder, this was my initial experience in being a part of such a loving and successful union.

As a child my father would not permit any cats living in our home but I always nurtured a great passion for both purebred and domestic felines. When I started my cattery with an unconditional love for all cats, I fell victim to wishful thinking. In the role of a new breeder I was dismayed to learn that the reverse would not always hold true. Not all my kittens loved me. Some kept their distance while others enjoyed being carried in my blouse and would take their turn seeking to be closer to me. It's always easier to love those that love us back, but a challenge to win the hearts of those that show indifference to our affections. Although the majority of kittens will respond to a gentle touch there are those that are waiting for the outstretched hand of the perfect owner selecting only them as their beloved choice. Much like children, kittens will instinctively respond to a situation and will immediately inform you of how they interpret your personal energy. Whereas many adult cats are willing to accept a pat and a kind word, kittens are often more selective with those they permit the same intimacy.

Such may explain the Feline Chameleon's concept of their universe. As small kittens they encounter large human creatures that move around the sheltered world of their nursery. These babies may appear aloof but truly have incredible radar for instinctively sensing the open heart of their imminent owner. Many buyers also respond in kind by immediately recognizing their perfect compliment in a Feline Chameleon. Roberto became the first of many kittens that waited for his owner and until the moment Fay held him he had only been comfortable with his mother and litter mates. He taught me one of my first valuable lessons as a breeder. There is a perfect cat for everyone and I learned to understand that even as small kittens they may not want to share their affections with their breeder.

There are also those Feline Chameleons that are late bloomers. These are the kittens that may be sociable in the cattery but once sold will totally change in their new home. It is amazing to watch their transformation as they slowly absorb the energy of their owner to later bloom in total contentment. I was acquainted with another friend who purchased a kitten from the same litter as my own Peter Pan male, Tally Ho. She named him Rufus and he was an average Himalayan kitten, preferring to play rather than being held. However he made a total transformation after living several months in her home.

My friend was a quiet unassuming person, but once she was at ease with company she could be great fun. Hence whenever I visited her home Rufus became equally withdrawn only displaying true contentment after I had taken my leave and he was alone with her. After being in Rufus' company for several hours he would eventually wander over to acknowledge my presence. Although he remained wary she informed me it was typical behavior for him with all visitors. For many years I was provided with the wonderful opportunity to study their unique relationship. As time passed he appeared to absorb my timid friend's energy, and that knowledge became a unique concept for me. Their relationship reminded me of a contented married couple. She preferred his company displaying little interest of ever remarrying, and their situation was ideal as they were totally content with each other. Their only area of disagreement involved a treasured chair in the living room. He was determined to claim it as his own, however it was also his mistress' favorite chair. A compromise was eventually met as he would permit her to sit in the beloved chair so long as he remained on her lap. It was a small price to pay for residing with a feline that provided such total devotion and loving companionship.

~~This mysterious mystical bundle of fur who won't come when you call him.~~ John Reynolds

My personal experience of residing with a female Feline Chameleon occurred with my first litter. I kept all but one kitten from a litter of five babies. I was blessed with an incredible stud male and three beautiful breeding females. The youngest of the litter was a small queen that presented an unknown challenge for me. This lovely girl was very difficult to name which was a problem I had never encountered before. She was a beautiful cat and was quite sociable however all the names I tried simply didn't describe her true personality. After several months and three attempts she finally found her own name and I was able to properly register her with my Cat Association. I named her Chloe after the interesting portrayal of Meg Tilly's unique character in the movie "The Big Chill." Chloe was a little off beat, beautiful but determined in every venture she chose to undertake. At the time this difficult to name kitten reflected those very same qualities. She was a tough little girl and held her own in the cattery, basking in an environment where she appeared content to affectionately interact with her many family members. Eventually she kittened well and following several litters she was petted out.

The woman who eventually adopted my sweet girl truly loved her unconditionally. I first met Penny when she accompanied her sister to visit my cattery seeking the perfect kitten. Unexpectantly Penny was drawn to Chloe and after an hour in her feline company expressed the desire to one day own her. It was decided that after my queen was finished in our breeding program I would contact her to discuss that possibility.

Following several years Penny was delighted to finally bring her chosen Persian home. It had initially taken months to name my kitten. When Penny finally adopted Chloe she decided the name didn't really compliment this female's inner beauty. With my encouragement Penny chose to rename her lovely little girl Samantha. Within a short period of time I finally realized that my inability to properly name Samantha was due to her status as a Feline Chameleon. Although I loved her and she was affectionate with me she was never truly meant to be my cat. I believe she knew she was misplaced. She was waiting for another person who would take my place and also become her human soul mate.

After settling into her new home this lovely Chameleon relaxed and began to mellow. Penny both adored and pampered her female's every whim and as a result Samantha lost the intensity of the personality she displayed in the cattery. The transformation was truly amazing as she softened and affectionately grew to mirror her very feminine owner. Penny and Samantha's relationship developed into the perfect compliment with each finding total fulfillment. Samantha had to wait many years for Penny and the intimate bond that eventually completed her personality. It became a loving match made in heaven and another lesson for me as a breeder in understanding the complexity of this unique Feline by Design personality.

~~A home without a cat, and a well-fed, well-petted, and properly revered cat, may be a perfect home, perhaps, but how can it prove it's title?~~ Mark Twain

Understanding the Felines by Design Principles

~~The really great thing about cats is their endless variety. One can pick a cat to fit almost any kind of decor, color, scheme, income, personality, mood. But under the fur, whatever color they may be, there still lies, essentially unchanged, one of the world's free souls.~~ Eric Gurney

Just as we are all individuals varying in personality, so too will the Felines by Design. My own cat Tally Ho is the epitome of the Peter Pan male. He does not alter nor assume any other designer personality. However you may have a Sophisticated Feral that occasionally appears out of character displaying traces of the Sociable Independent. When you least expect her to be sociable with visitors she will comfortably make her presence known. Many Sophisticated Ferals once encountering their human soul mate will assume total peace with their place in the world. As they mature and their trust becomes secure they may display unaccustomed characteristics which are truly delightful for their owner.

The Felines by Design principles will greatly assist those searching for a cat who both touches their heart and meets their emotional needs. For those who must work long hours and spend a limited period of time at home they should seek a cat who will be comfortable with their lifestyle. Conversely, for those seeking a feline who will remain by their side as they work from home the same designer personality may be most inappropriate. Although some felines truly follow their designer personality other cats will be a blending of several personalities with much depending on their owners and living situations.

Domestic kittens can vary greatly in personality due to their diverse genetic backgrounds even when they are born within the same litter. When seeking a compatible kitten, unless you have been exposed to the Felines by Design principles it may come down to luck of the draw. If you are selecting a kitten from a home raised litter, question the queen's owner regarding the various personalities. With domestic litters the Felines by Design principles are especially important, as it is difficult to judge personalities from observation alone. The kittens' caregiver will be exposed to information that is only learned from living in the same home as the litter.

Although some purebred breeds are quieter by nature, each individual kitten has a unique soul and perspective of the world. Siamese kittens are wonderful company but some have extremely loud voices when they need to communicate with their owners. Some Himalayans may have also inherited this trait. For example, no queen ever called quite so loudly as my own Seal Point Himalayan Caterina. Persians are quieter by nature and with their cobby legs are limited in their ability to jump onto window ledges from the floor. However not every Persian will be a quiet feline and not every Himalayan will call loudly when seeking their needs be met. The selection of a kitten is often an instinctive choice. However it can be difficult to cope with a feline that does not respond with affection or compliment your own personality. The Felines by Design personalities presented in this publication have been selected as they specifically enjoy residing in smaller spaces.

When searching for a purebred it is important to research the breed that you are most attracted to and select a kitten with the guidance of the breeder. With the selection of a domestic feline it is better to question the caregiver regarding each kitten in the litter. From the information provided by the breeder or caregiver, select the kitten that appears to be the Feline by

Design best suited for your personal compatibility and living arrangements. There are numerous questions you may need answered to guide you through this process with either the breeder or caregiver. It is important to understand and interpret their responses, and these guidelines are provided in Volumes 2 and 3 of the Felines by Design series[3]. These will assist both the purebred and domestic cat lover in selecting their perfect kitten.

~~The cat does not offer services. The cat offers himself. Of course he wants care and shelter. You don't buy love for nothing. Like all pure creatures, cats are practical. ~~
William Seward Burroughs

---

[3] Felines by Design series: Volume 2: Insider's Guide to Buying Purebred Kittens, Volume 3: Insider's Guide to Selecting Domestic Felines

The Feline in Grief

~~No Heaven will ever be Heaven for me; Unless my cats are there to welcome me~~ Unknown

Whereas many of us have experienced the devastating loss of a beloved cat there are also felines who will sadly experience loss through the death of their owners. Following requests on our Confessions of a Cat Breeder web site, it was decided to provide information to assist those caring for felines coping with this difficult situation. *The Feline in Grief* is being presented in abridged form from Volumes 2 and 3 of the Felines by Design series. Those residing in a pet restricted residence often inherit cats. Therefore it was felt that this publication should also address this sensitive issue.

There are many aspects of feline grief that are never considered until circumstances in life present this difficult situation. Felines will grieve their companion cat's death and will also deeply grieve their human soul mate when such a loss occurs. Felines will grieve during the dissolution of a marriage when their owners decide to separate. Felines will also sadly grieve a child who upon maturity will depart from the family home leaving their beloved cat behind. As a Feline Behavior Consultant I have dealt with various aspects of feline grief and learned through trial and error those methods that worked and others that were less effective. As every feline is different so are the various methods that may assist their owner during the feline grieving process.

Felines emotionally experience abandonment, fear and loss not unlike what we must process ourselves while we are coping with grief. However, whereas we understand the nature of our loss a cat simply knows they have been abandoned. Without an ability to comprehend the true nature of their owner's death they will additionally internalize the many changes that will quickly follow in their lives.

Even with the loss of one owner when a feline has been living with a couple, there are additional challenges they must process. Although changes in residence are not always necessary they are left residing with a grieving marriage partner. Cats are not only grieving themselves but may be the surviving partner's sole comfort. This feline will also witness their owner's change in personality and emotional discomfort on a daily basis.

Many felines also display symptoms of grief when a beloved family member leaves home for college. In the event a couple ends their relationship and separates what happens to a feline that has loved both owners and additionally must process moving to a second residence? A feline will become depressed when coping with unaccustomed or erratic emotions from their owner and like a sponge will absorb the same disturbed energy. Unless these situations are addressed with understanding and care many felines will react by displaying behavioral problems. Quite often such problems are temporary and will subside when the family adjusts to a new pattern of normalcy.

Personally I have also experienced several of these difficult situations. Dustin, my first domestic cat changed residences with me while I was grieving the loss of a long-term relationship. He was an exceptionally sensitive feline and provided emotional comfort while I struggled through numerous stressful changes occurring in my life. Years later I understood with compassion the reasons why some buyers desired to purchase my kittens following an ending to their marriage. A kitten is a new beginning and assists an owner to focus on their feline's needs rather than reliving emotional baggage from their recent past.

~~I love cats because I enjoy my home; and little by little, they become its visible soul~~ Jean Cocteau

Ten years ago I inherited two domestic Calico cats from a dear friend who died suddenly following a brief illness. She was greatly comforted during her last days by my promise and reassurance that her cats would always remain in my care. I was not prepared however for the duration and depth of their collective grief for their lost owner.

When Thelma became ill she shipped Misty and Christy 3,000 miles across the country to stay in my care. Thelma dearly loved her cats, however even after settling into my home they exhibited unusally high levels of stress and were severely overweight. I quickly adjusted their diet and with time came to better understand my new charges. Thelma arrived several weeks later and lived with me until her hospitalization became a necessity. She had never owned cats before having only shared her home with family dogs. Thelma attempted to control her felines in the same manner as some owners discipline their dogs. She constantly raised her voice and gave them taps on their bottoms in an attempt to curb their normal feline behavior.

After several weeks had passed I shared my observations of the Calicos' neurotic behavior with her. I then provided advice that resulted in the desired behavioral management she needed. Without the stress from repetitive loud verbal discipline her felines slowly began to adapt and change. Thelma told me that she had a better understanding of her cats in the several months we shared together than in the three years she had previously owned them. She was deeply sincere and it touched my heart that she shared this information with me while she was dying. However Thelma's Calicos still refused to acknowledge me even months prior to her death. Not only did they not appreciate my efforts to make their lives more comfortable, but they also refused my many attempts to initiate a relationship with them. I was simply put in my place and was totally ignored. Although they would permit me to pet them on occasion their affections remained solely reserved for their owner.

I told my friend to not worry and that I would care for her cats for the duration of their young lives. However as the days passed I wondered if my decision had been a wise one. Several days following Thelma's death her beloved Calicos remained confused and unsettled. I was unsure of how to comfort them while they were in emotional bereavement. We were all grieving her loss, however Misty and Christy were only aware that she was no longer available to love and care for them. The girls needed space and privacy therefore it only made sense to empty all of Thelma's clothing onto the bed in her room. I provided food and water and a litter box for the girls' private use in the bedroom Thelma had occupied while living in my home.

The two Calicos had freedom of movement within the house but rarely left Thelma's room. For three weeks the girls preferred to be left in peace and quiet, and slept on their deceased owner's clothing covering the entire bed. It was only after a month had passed and as I noticed the perfume from Thelma's clothing had begun to fade that the girls would leave the room for longer periods of time. Eventually when her scent was no longer present even to a cat's sensitive nose they finally accepted their beloved owner was truly gone.

Although one of the Calicos appeared more accepting of me than the other, I witnessed distinct changes in their perception of my role within their lives. Felines place great trust in their sense of smell. Once Thelma's scent had totally faded from her clothing they quickly lost interest in her bedroom. After they completely abandoned the clothing I started occasionally using Thelma's perfume when I handled her girls. I believe this also assisted in their grieving process and understanding that I would now take her place and provide love and care for them.

Although I have lost one of the Calico girls back to Thelma I still deeply cherish the surviving sister. Christy was the more aloof of the two cats but she was also the Sociable Independent Feline by Design that was totally devoted to Thelma. Once she transferred her loyalty to me I was rewarded with a feline's love only equal to that of my long lost beloved Feline Soul Mate Caterina. After Thelma's passing I changed her name from Christy to Chrissy as I needed to make her my own cat. I believe softening her name may have had some reflection on her bonding and developing a relationship with me. With the passing years Chrissy has developed diabetes but she remains youthful and still plays like a young kitten. She also loves the office chair where she can keep an eye on my work. It's difficult to connect her to the younger and more aloof Calico I was introduced to so many years ago. I've never regretted my promise to Thelma because in the end I was actually giving myself a gift in the form of a feline treasure of love and affection.

Felines will grieve but they also respond with love and kindness to those who are willing to open their heart and homes to them. I believe a cat knows when you have over extended yourself to make their lives better. The rewards are numerous for those who are willing to love a feline who has lost their owner. Your commitment to a cat with unconditional love is well worth your time and effort. In life you only keep what you give away, and as a result your life will be enriched in more ways than you may believe possible.

~~I believe cats to be spirits come to earth. A cat, I am sure, could walk on a cloud without coming through.~~ Jules Verne

Coping with Stress

Keep in mind the delicate balance between your cat's emotional health and your own personal stress level. It is wise to monitor your feline's stress while managing the stress in your own life as well. Do something special for yourself on a regular basis. For some people physical activity such as jogging or yoga is effective, while others prefer weekly massage or Reiki treatments. By incorporating such an activity in your weekly routine it will develop into a personal method of projecting positive energy. For those preferring exercise you will also reap the rewards of being a physically active person. You will shed the accumulation of stress in everyday life as well as the stress of hiding your cat. Live a balanced life by controlling your own stress and therefore controlling the stress your cat absorbs through you.

In managing your cat's stress, take into consideration that you are the center of your feline's world. If you are a person concerned with your career and working long days it is unfair to leave your cat alone for many hours. Take into consideration not only your professional work but also your social life. If you prefer an active social life then you might consider having more of a social life at home. You may save money and your cat will benefit emotionally from the interaction with your many friends and family.

If you explore the quieter personalities we have suggested chances are you will have a contented feline and therefore a successful experience in hiding your cat from the Landlord. It is best to find a cat that is sociable but does not mind some periods of isolation. As a breeder I was able to select just the right kitten for each situation. Often the lead kitten in a litter is comfortable in a smaller space where he spends his days alone. Should you be considering two kittens a perfect compliment is a litter mate combination of sister and brother or sister and sister.   A brother and brother relationship may work as well, but only if they were exceptionally close as litter mates. If you are fortunate to encounter a breeder in whom you are able to confide your intentions allow her to guide you in the careful selection of your kittens using the Felines by Design principles.

Worry... Borrowing
Tomorrow's Trouble Before It's Time

The word 'worry' comes from an old Anglo-Saxon verb 'wyrgan' meaning to choke or strangle. World-renowned best selling author Norman Vincent Peale said that worry frustrates one's best functioning. In other words worry and anxiety choke the joy out of living. There is a difference between concern or healthy worry and anxious worry. It is normal to worry and be concerned if we lose our job, when our children are not home at night and have not called to tell us where they are, or when we are having marital or other relational conflicts. The problem is when the worry is out of proportion to what has happened, or when the worry causes us to live in a constant state of anxiety.

When I worked for the Government I cut an article from a weekly newsletter that was circulated for the employees in my office. The short article outlined the meaning of worry and the percentage of worrying that we do in our lives. I worried to such an extent that I would suffer with severe anxiety attacks and greatly needed this information. I had the article laminated and reduced to credit card size so I could keep it in my purse at all times. I kept that reminder with me for over 20 years until I met someone who needed it more than I did and passed it along to her.

- **40% of our worries simply NEVER happen**
- **30% concern issues from our past**
- **12% concern people of importance to us**
- **10% concern our health**
- **Thus only 8% of our concerns are <u>truly</u> valid**

For thirty years I worried that we would be discovered and I would lose my cats. However following many sleepless nights it proved to be that 40% of worrying which never happened. My core belief is that everything in our lives occurs for a reason. I learned through therapy to trust in the Universe and to also accept the truth behind the concept that 40% of my worries would never happen. Worry is truly a habit, and if we worry then perhaps it won't happen. I would submit that even the 8% considered valid really isn't worth the energy of worry. A day of worry is more exhausting than a day of work. We become so absorbed in worrying about yesterday or tomorrow that we forget about enjoying today.

Dale Carnegie, best selling author of "How to Win Friends and Influence People" and "How to Stop Worrying and Start Living," credits Willis H. Carrier with the following jewel of thought:

- **Analyze the situation honestly and figure out what is the worst possible thing that could happen**

- **Prepare yourself mentally to accept the worst, if necessary**

- **Then calmly try to improve upon the worst, which you have already agreed mentally to accept**

I realized the worry and anxiety in my life were symptoms which had been triggered from unresolved issues in my past. My worry and anxiety were due to a childhood of fears and problems which my conscious mind had long since forgotten. It sounds so simple but is truly a complex situation for many people who are prone to fear and anxiety. In my situation the worry I felt while hiding my cattery was primarily based on fear and uncertainty. Anxiety is caused when we think we might lose something important to us. For thirty years I lived in fear and surrounded myself with worry because I simply could not accept losing my cats.

To worry about a situation we cannot change is a terrible waste of emotional energy. According to renowned lecturer and writer Leo Buscaglia:

> ## Worry never robs tomorrow of its sorrow, it only saps today of its joy.

For some readers the entire concept of hiding a cat is too stressful to even consider. However for others, such as myself, to live without my beloved cats would have created a life too stressful to be enjoyed. Therefore I simply trusted in the Universe to protect us and did everything in my power to maintain our privacy.

All the work to hide my cats, the money spent on rent and the long hours I worked to support my family were worth the stress and even the worry. If I was able to go back in time, the one thing I would change is to have more faith in the process of incorporating positive energy into my life. I would have saved myself years of anxiety and worry.

An interesting observation for me personally is that anxiety in my body centers in my throat with an inability to swallow. For many years during periods of stress my throat appeared to swell and I would literally choke on my food. Hence I am the living example of the word 'worry' as noted above which means to choke or strangle.

<u>Conclusion</u>

"It's the character that's the strongest that God gives the most challenges to, and you can take that as a compliment." I have gathered several such passages of wisdom and used them in my life during anxious periods of time. I have also used every opportunity to pass the strength such passages offer to others whose lives may appear almost too difficult to bear. If you are deciding to introduce a kitten into your home you will also be embracing some fear of the unknown. There's the anxiety that your Landlord may possibly discover your cat, however you will also be embracing the great joy your feline will bring into your home.

Through the many interviews I conducted, not one cat owner regretted their decision to hide their cat from the Landlord. Although it was a personal decision for each cat lover, once made each caregiver had few regrets. Despite my own circumstances I would not have made any changes either. The time I shared with my beloved Caterina was priceless and worth any difficulties I encountered while attempting to keep my many breeding felines both content and hidden.

Many are familiar with the quote from William Shakespeare's Hamlet, "To Thine Own Self Be True." Everyone has a different concept of this saying but during my life I've only taken the wrong path when I haven't been true to my own heart or followed my deepest instincts. To have not bred my cats despite hiding an entire cattery from my Landlord would have been untrue to myself. I would have never made it through those difficult years of too much work and not enough money. I was rich with life because my heart was full.

~~There are two means of refuge from the miseries of life; music and cats.~~ Albert Schweitzer

Publications from Jasmine Kinnear

Titles from the Felines by Design Series

Vol. 1: Proven Marketing Tips for the Successful Cat Breeder
Vol. 2: Insider's Guide to Buying Purebred Kittens
Vol. 3: Insider's Guide to Selecting Domestic Felines
Vol. 4: Insider's Guide to Starting & Managing a Cattery

Additional volumes in this series will be forthcoming.

For more information please visit our web site:

www.confessionsofacatbreeder.com

How to Contact Jasmine Kinnear

Should you have any questions regarding this publication, feline behavior issues, managing or marketing your cattery we welcome your inquiries on Jasmine Kinnear's **Confessions of a Cat Breeder** web site. Please sign the Guest Book then explore our Feline Message Forum, breeding tips and feline stories. We further welcome our readers who wish to share their own personal experiences with their favorite feline.

www.confessionsofacatbreeder.com

Glossary

The following definitions are provided to assist all cat owners. You may even discover a few jewels of wisdom.

Cat Association: The Cat Fanciers Association (CFA), The International Cat Association (TICA), and the American Cat Fancier's Association (ACFA), to name just a few, are the professional Cat Associations known worldwide. These organizations register catteries and purebred litters. In order to be a 'registered breeder', a cattery name must be accepted by a chosen Association. Each individual cat's bloodline must be proven by registered pedigree if not already registered within the chosen Association.

Each Association monitors the results from professional judging within their registered cat shows. Every breeder anxiously watches the mail at year end to be notified where their campaigned feline star will show in the Association's 'Year Book'.

To learn more you may visit each association's respective web site below:

The Cat Fanciers Association (CFA):
   http://www.cfainc.org
The International Cat Association (TICA):
   http://www.tica.org
American Cat Fancier's Association (ACFA):
   http://www.acfacats.com

Cattery: A cattery is the place where cats are bred and the resulting litters are born. Some catteries may become quite large with the cats residing in a separate building on the breeder's property. In many cases, the larger catteries cage their stud males, queens and litters to make the handling of so many cats and kittens easier. Some kittens live their first few months with little human contact. This may result in a fearful kitten when it is finally released into the buyer's new home.

Many breeders prefer to keep their catteries to a moderate size and provide a home-raised environment. The 'stud male' will have to be caged. However 'queens' and litters will have the freedom of the home and be handled by the family on a daily basis. It is far easier for a kitten to make the transition into a buyer's home if raised lovingly in the breeder's residence.

Chirping, Vocalizing: Purebred and domestic felines both male and female love to 'chirp' and communicate by using different pitches of vocalizations with their owners. Should you own a feline that enjoys vocalizing it becomes one of the most intimate acts you can share with them.

There is an entire vocabulary behind your feline's attempt to communicate with you. It can be a wonderful challenge to identify your cat's speech patterns. If you are blessed with such a cat, listen then share the conversation by responding. Your cat will enjoy your human attempts to communicate on their level and the bond between you will become even stronger.

Cremation: Cremation is a private matter that is rarely discussed until a loss occurs and a decision must be made. Many pet lovers feel that the separation of burial is too final so cremation becomes an important issue.

Before surrendering your pet please note that crematoriums, unless instructed otherwise will cremate many cats and dogs simultaneously. Each owner is then given an urn of accumulated ashes. If you wish to receive only your own cat's ashes it is essential that you request a 'private' cremation. Although a little more costly for many feline lovers in bereavement it is the only option.

Many animal hospitals will charge an additional service fee for handling these stressful details when such a loss occurs. However if you have a family friend who is able to deal directly with the crematorium and provide the transportation of your beloved pet, there will be less expense.

I have spoken to many feline lovers who have requested that their own ashes be scattered with their beloved cat's ashes. I made the same request several years ago when the idea was presented to me by my son Mark when he was six-years-old. For some reason the thought is comforting and as I correspond with other cat lovers I realize I'm not the first to have such a wish.

Cupboard Loving Kitty: This phrase could be equally applied to any healthy teenage boy who empties the refrigerator as quickly as his parents fill it.   Although I've never met a Cupboard Loving Kitty I do own a Sociable Independent feline who demonstrates the same passion for my company as she does for her favorite dinner. It is a myth that cats only love their owners so long as they are fed. Although the road to a man's heart may be through his stomach, a cat shows far greater discretion when selecting the caregiver she loves.

Domestic Cat: It is always disturbing when some owners refer to their beloved pets as 'just' a domestic. Domestic cats appear to have longer life spans than many purebreds and are just as beloved to their families.

A domestic cat is more often than not the result of a backyard breeding encounter. Domestics are fortunate to not be as restricted by a limited gene pool as are many purebred felines. Provided a domestic is offered a good diet and resides in a loving inside environment they can bless their owners by living a long and healthy life. When the sire of a domestic litter is a 'feral cat' his kittens may inherit his wild nature.

Felines by Design: A breeder who has spent time with her kittens is able to successfully match kittens with the right buyer. A **Kitten by Design** shares similar characteristics as the owner. When a perfect match occurs a **Kitten by Design** develops into a **Feline by Design**. Owners will proclaim an amazing lifetime blending of souls with their cat. In future sales many buyers will only accept a feline if it has been proclaimed by the breeder as the perfect **Kitten by Design** selected just for them. Only a **Feline by Design** can truly become their owner's Feline Soul Mate as they are eternally bonded.

Feral Cat: A true feral cat is one born in the wild with little or no human contact. The feral cat has a shortened lifespan and usually lives and breeds in the wild totally independent of human care.

Fight or Flight: When felines are confronted by a sudden loud noise or the encounter of an unknown cat they experience a rapid rush of adrenaline. There is no decision made as the reaction is both primeval and associated with the specific designer personality. They will take instant <u>flight</u> and quickly hide or face their adversary and assume the posture of a cat facing a <u>fight</u> to the death.

One personal experience with Fight or Flight involved two of my favorite stud cats. A queen was being courted by Spencer in his huge inside/outside luxury nook while Chadwick was enjoying some free liberty exploring the cattery. As everything appeared in order and with all cattery duties completed, I returned upstairs to work in the kitchen. Within five minutes I heard the distinct and deadly "beware" growls of two males positioning themselves for a fight to the death. I raced down to the cattery and discovered Chadwick had cornered Spencer in his nook. Both cats were reluctantly positioning themselves ready to defend the honor of the calling queen. Either I hadn't latched Spencer's door properly or Chadwick had pried open the base of the door to gain entry.

I have known breeders to use brooms, spray bottles of water and other assorted methods to separate two studs in a fight to the death. However I was fortunate as I knew the true temperament of both my breeding males. I'd never been placed in such a situation before with only moments separating a vicious battle over a female. In true Bewitching Goddess style, Candace positioned herself to watch the battle between the two males for her honor. I knew neither of my boys wanted to fight however both defiantly stood their ground defending the established macho male stud code of honor.

I took my place in front of the males and using the full length of my housecoat, simply separated them with my robe blocking their sight of each other. They both immediately withdrew and it appeared to me that they were grateful as neither wanted to engage in battle. I'd like to believe that a Dignified Gentleman and a Lovable Teddy Bear would never have fought to the death. However when a breeding queen and two stud males are involved anything may happen. The situation required instinctive action and quick thinking in order to prevent injury or a possible fight to the death.

I turned and picked up Chadwick quickly leaving Spencer's nook. Before placing him back into his own nook Chadwick affectionately nuzzled me under my chin. He was obviously aware that he'd been rescued from an unpleasant situation. I then returned to Spencer and hugged him as well thanking him for his patience with the younger male. I'd like to believe that Spencer as my Dignified Gentleman would never have harmed Chadwick. However that day Spencer let it be known that his nook was to be respected as his castle. Chadwick must have learned the lesson as he never again found his way back into the senior stud male's domain.

Kitten Fever: This condition is known as an uncontrollable urge to have a kitten from any breeder at any price. Good sense flies out the window and the buyer follows their heart with little regard for their personal financial circumstances. Used car dealers know the look of a first time buyer and may take advantage of the situation. However a good breeder proceeds with kindness and caution without exploiting the buyer's vulnerability. This condition is also known to affect those viewing domestic litters.

Multi-cat Household: The true feline lover always has room for one more cat. Jasmine believes that although problems occur while personalities adjust to one another, every cat should have a compatible feline companion. When three cats or more are residing in your home, you are truly blessed with belonging to a multi-cat household.

Nursery Nook: I had three nursery nooks in my bedroom. My newborn birthing nook was fully enclosed and ran the entire length of my six foot dresser. Queens delivered inside the nursery nook on my dresser or if it was their preference, in a cardboard box cushioned with sanitary liners that was placed on my bed. Once kittens became mobile they were moved into a corner of my large empty bedroom closet that provided space for safe exploration. Some queens preferred a deluxe box while others loved a warm soft blanket and nestled their kittens safely into a protected corner.

Pet Out: This term is used when breeders have decided to give a queen or stud male away to a home where they will be loved and well cared for. It is best to leave the feline with the cattery veterinarian for altering and the new owner to accept the feline after the procedure has been completed. This is an ideal situation for seniors who may wish to have a purebred feline without the work of a kitten. The breeder will have an intimate knowledge of the feline and play matchmaker by successfully placing the cat in the right home. Depending on the circumstances the breeder may request a nominal fee for the cost of altering or simply gift the feline to the new owner.

Proven Male: When a young male sucessfully sires a litter, he is known as a proven male.

Queen or Dam: A grown female cat is referred to as a queen. The mother of a litter of kittens is known as the dam of the litter. The term dam applies to both purebred and domestic queens who have given birth to a litter of kittens.

Registered Breeder: In most Cat Associations the breeder is given the same registration number as her cattery. When the cattery name is accepted and registered the breeder submitting the cattery for registration is automatically registered as well.

Spraying: Male cats spray leaving their individual odor to mark their territory. Some stud males are chronic sprayers while others seldom spray. The spray scent from a male cat is unmistakable. Some 'whole' males are non-sprayers. These precious males bless their catteries by never leaving their personal calling card inside or outside the confines of their cages.
  A female cat may spray urine against walls or furniture during a heat cycle or when overstressed. This sometimes occurs when there is limited space in an overcrowded cattery.

Stud Male or Sire: This term only refers to breeding male cats. Breeding males are incredibly loving but may also be difficult to handle.

Stud Nook: Stud nooks are homes for the resident breeding males and must be spacious and cleaned frequently. Several of my stud males had expansive inside/outside nooks with ample space to exercise. Each male was provided with continuous entertainment by having access to a large enclosed outside balcony.

Whole Cat: An uncastrated cat is also referred to as a whole cat. Male or female, domestic or purebred, whole cats are ruled by their hormones. When your cat is altered, you are blessed with a more secure, non-territorial feline that will readily bond with family members.

Check with your veterinarian regarding the correct age to alter. Queens should be altered prior to their first heat. Males should be altered before they start spraying.

You Only Keep What You Give Away: Several times while writing this book I have felt the need to use this favorite expression. The concept of You Only Keep What You Give Away has brought many personal blessings into my life and I believe it deserves to be acknowledged. For many years I have drawn strength from this philosophy and several times I have been astonished by it's accuracy.

At first the simplicity of this concept appeared a little unnerving. I soon discovered that my belief was not only true but also rather simple. When you give from the heart without expecting anything in return your initial act of kindness will always be returned to you. Whether that generosity be in a monetary sense or by a simple gesture of kindness, whatever I gave always came back to me. I've always received the money I gave or was the recipient of an act of kindness in return. For some reason my generosity was always returned when I least expected it and truly needed the assistance.

Index

Dignified Gentleman, 57-62, 70
Dingman, John, 45
Domestic cat, 116, 118, 133
Douglas, Auriel, 89
Duplexes, 12, 34, 35

E
Engram, Frank, 107

F
Feline Chameleon, 107-113
Feline Soul Mate, 55, 84, 110, 121, 134
Feline Zeus, 89-92, 95, 100
Felines by Design, 11, 39, 41, 54, 55, 61, 73, 78, 79, 100-105, 114-117, 123, 134
Feral, 82-85, 99, 104, 134, 136
Fight or flight, 73, 80, 134
Fleischer, Lenore, 107

G
Gallico, Paul, 36, 61
Gautier, Theophile, 73, 93
Gray, Charlotte, 38
Grief, 11, 19, 77, 117-119
Gurney, Eric, 114

H
Hall, Bonni Elizabeth, 64
Hamlet, 128
Hawk, Dr. Larry, 29
Head cat, 68, 81, 86
Heinlein, Richard A., 15
Hemingway, Ernest, 20, 39
Herriot, James, 48

High Rise Syndrome (HRS), 28-30
Hohoff, Tay, 40
Hollyn, Lynn, 100
Hotel, 51, 52
Hotel Kitty, 67
Humane Society of the United States (HSUS), 48

I
Ivory, Lesley Anne, 106

J
Jewett, Sarah Orne, 86

K
Kinnear, Isabell Ann, 102
Kitten fever, 79, 136

L
Lady of Distinction, 61-64
Laing, Dilys, 101
Lead kitten, 103, 108, 122
Legal ownership, 27
Lifestyle, 10, 17, 54, 114
Litter box, 28, 38, 41-49, 52, 58, 80, 102, 104, 120
Lovable Teddy Bear, 93-96, 99, 101, 102

M
Manager, 15, 17-20, 24, 33
McCrohan, Donna, 78
McDonough, Susan, D.V.M, 74
Mery,Fernand, 13
Millen, Susanne, 44
Montaigne, 67

Multi-cat household, 79, 81, 136

N
Nichols, Beverly, 65
Nisbet, Rosemary, 77
Non-aggressive, 78, 80, 81
Nursery nook, 103, 136

O
Ownership, 12, 27, 40

P
Peale, Norman Vincent, 124
Perfect Condo Kitty, 11, 33, 54, 55, 59, 63, 65, 82
Pet out, 137
Pet store, 23, 24, 27, 82
Peter Pan, 73-80, 94, 100, 111, 114
Peterson, Kathrine Palmer, 34
Powers, Helen, 67
Precious Treasure, 73, 78-81, 100
Privacy, 12, 15-22, 28, 31-33, 36, 45, 53, 120, 127
Proven male, 137

Q
Queen, 13, 39, 71-75, 81-88, 91-96, 100-107, 112-115, 132, 137

R
Rabinovitch, Donna J., 81, 101
Rainbow Bridge, 100
Rampa, T Iobsang, 61

Registered breeder, 131, 137
Reiki Treatments, 122
Rental agencies, 17
Rental management company, 31, 32
Reynard, Jules, 33
Reynolds, John, 112

S
Sarton, May, 31
Schweitzer, Albert, 128
Scratching pole, 17, 34, 36, 41, 63, 70, 77, 83, 91, 97
Sebaceous gland, 74
Security, 16, 20, 22, 33, 41, 42, 59, 68-76, 87
Shakespeare, William, 128
Sire, 72, 75, 85, 133, 138
Smaller homes, 9, 34, 59, 63
Smaller spaces, 9, 11, 40, 55, 70, 94, 104, 108, 115
Sociable Independent, 63-73, 94, 114, 121
Sophisticated Feral, 44, 69, 81-86, 90, 94, 114
SPCA, San Francisco, 48
Spiritual, 9, 58, 101, 103
Spraying, 137
Stress, 9-15, 24-28, 35-38, 42, 46, 58, 80, 118-122, 127, 133
Stud male, 13, 57, 71-75, 91-99, 112, 132, 138
Stud nook, 138
Symons, Arthur, 57

T
The Big Chill, 112

www.ingramcontent.com/pod-product-compliance
Lightning Source LLC
LaVergne TN
LVHW011356080426
835511LV00005B/309